The Global Public
Management Revolution

CENTER
for **PUBLIC**
SERVICE

The Brookings Institution established the Center for Public Service in 1999 to improve the odds that America's most talented citizens will choose careers in the public service. Toward that goal, the center is committed to rigorous research and practical recommendations for making public service more attractive, be it in traditional government settings, nonprofit agencies, or the growing number of private firms that provide services once delivered inside government. As the center's logo suggests, the single-sectored, government-centered public service of the 1970s has been replaced by the multisectored, highly mobile public service of today. The center was created to track the rise of this new public service, while making sure that both government and the nonprofit sector can compete for their fair share of talent in an ever-tightening labor market.

As part of this effort, the Center for Public Service is committed to publishing timely reports on the state of the public service. These reports, which vary in length from short reports to books, attempt to lay the foundation for long-needed policy reforms. Because these reports are designed to move quickly into publication, some will not be verified to the same level of detail as other Brookings publications. As with all Brookings publications, the judgments, conclusions, and recommendations presented in any individual study are solely those of the author or authors and should not be attributed to the trustees, officers, or other staff members of the institution.

DONALD F. KETTL

The Global Public Management Revolution

A REPORT ON THE TRANSFORMATION OF GOVERNANCE

BROOKINGS INSTITUTION PRESS
Washington, D.C.

Copyright © 2000
THE BROOKINGS INSTITUTION
1775 Massachusetts Avenue, N.W., Washington, D.C. 20036
www.brookings.edu

Library of Congress Cataloging-in-Publication data

Kettl, Donald F.
The global public management revolution: a report on the
transformation of governance / Donald F. Kettl
    p.   cm.
Includes bibliographical references and index.
ISBN 0-8157-4917-1 (pb : acid-free)
    1. Administrative agencies—United States—Management.   2.
Administrative agencies—New Zealand—Management.   I. Title:
Management reform for the twenty-first century.   II. Title.

JK421 .K48 2000   00-008351
352.3'67—dc21   CIP

9 8 7 6 5 4 3 2 1

The paper used in this publication meets minimum requirements of the
American National Standard for Information Sciences—Permanence of Paper
for Printed Library Materials: ANSI Z39.48-1984.

Typeset in Sabon

Composition by R. Lynn Rivenbark
Macon, GA

Printed by
Automated Graphics Systems
White Plains, Maryland

Foreword

Over the last two decades, governments around the world have launched ambitious efforts to reform the way they manage their programs. Citizens everywhere have demanded smaller, cheaper, more effective governments. They have also asked for more programs and better services. To resolve this paradox, governments have experimented with scores of ideas to be more productive, to improve performance, and to reduce costs.

In this report of the Center for Public Service, which continues the work of the former Center for Public Management in a new home, Donald F. Kettl surveys the global public management revolution. He charts the major strategies, including New Zealand's "new public management," the U.S. effort at "reinventing government," and related efforts in developed and developing nations around the world. Kettl finds that this movement has revolved around six core ideas: the search for greater productivity; more public reliance on private markets; a stronger orientation toward service; more decentralization from national to subnational governments; increased capacity to devise and track public policy; and tactics to enhance accountability for results.

Most of all, Kettl finds, the reform movement has been about governance: public efforts to strengthen the connections between government and the mechanisms, both in government and in civil society, that are responsible for how well government works. The movement has built on the notion that good governance—a sorting out of mission, role, capacity, and relationships—is a necessary (if insufficient) condition for economic prosperity and social stability.

The report draws on discussions at the Global Forum on Reinventing Government, held in Washington, January 1–15, 1999. The forum was cosponsored by the Innovations in American Government Program, Kennedy School of Government, Harvard University; the Innovations in Government Program, the Ford Foundation; the World Bank; the Inter-American Development Bank; the Organization for Economic Cooperation and Development; the National Partnership for Reinventing Government; the Office of Management and Budget; the Brookings Institution; and the United States Information Agency. Kettl is grateful to these organizations for their assistance and to the comments that many of their officials made on earlier drafts of this report. He particularly thanks the Ford Foundation, which funded the Center for Public Management before it was merged into the Center for Public Service, for its support of his work.

The views expressed in this book are those of the author and should not be ascribed to any of the institutions acknowledged above or to the trustees, officers, or other staff members of the Brookings Institution.

MICHAEL H. ARMACOST
President

Washington, D.C.
March 2000

Contents

CHAPTER ONE

Foundations
of Reform

Since the 1980s a global reform movement in public management has been vigorously under way. The movement has been global in two senses. First, it has spread around the world to nations including Mongolia, Sweden, New Zealand, and the United States. Second, it has been sweeping in scope. Governments have used management reform to reshape the role of the state and its relationship with citizens. Some nations, such as the United States, have been inveterate reformers.

The movement has been striking because of the number of nations that have taken up the reform agenda in such a short time and because of how similar their basic strategies have been. In general it has embodied six core characteristics:[1]

—*Productivity:* How can governments produce more services with less tax money? Citizens everywhere have demanded a rollback in their taxes but have scarcely reduced their taste for government services. Governments have had to find ways to squeeze more services from the same— or smaller—revenue base.

—*Marketization:* How can government use market-style incentives to root out the pathologies of government bureaucracy? Some governments have privatized extensively by selling public enterprises, whereas others have relied heavily on nongovernmental partners for service delivery. In both cases, they struggled to change the driving incentives of public policy. Underlying all these tactics is a basic strategy: Replace traditional bureaucratic command-and-control mechanisms with market strategies, and then rely on these strategies to change the behavior of program managers.

—*Service orientation:* How can government better connect with citizens? Public opinion polls show that public trust in government institutions has declined and that many citizens believe that government programs are unresponsive. To make programs more responsive, governments have tried to turn their service delivery systems upside down. Instead of designing programs from the point of view of service providers (especially government officials) and managing them through existing bureaucratic structures, reformers have tried to put citizens (as service recipients) first. In some cases, this strategy has meant giving citizens choice among alternative service systems. In other cases, it has meant training program managers to focus on service. Markets naturally provide consumers with choice. Government reformers have used market mechanisms to give citizens the same choice—or at least to encourage a customer-oriented approach in government services.

—*Decentralization:* How can government make programs more responsive and effective? In many nations, the reform strategy has decentralized many programs to lower levels of government. In some federal systems (for example, Australia, Canada, Switzerland, and the United States), this strategy has meant shifting power within the system. In other nations, it has meant transferring more service delivery responsibilities to local governments as an additional tactic to make government more responsive. Some governments also have decentralized responsibility within public agencies to give frontline managers greater incentive and ability to respond to citizens' needs.

—*Policy:* How can government improve its capacity to devise and track policy? Many governments, following the lead of New Zealand, have quite explicitly separated government's role as purchaser of services (its policy function) from its role in providing them (its service-delivery function). These governments have sought to improve the efficiency of service delivery, which might or might not remain in the hands of government, while improving their purchasing capacity.

—*Accountability for results:* How can governments improve their ability to deliver what they promise? Governments have tried to replace top-down, rule-based accountability systems with bottom-up, results-driven systems. They sought to focus on outputs and outcomes instead of processes and structures.

Painted with the broadest brush, these reforms sought to replace traditional rule-based, authority-driven processes with market-based, competition-driven tactics. Indeed, many nations with substantial state-owned enterprises (such as telephone companies, airlines, and power generation companies) explicitly applied the market model to them. But the global reform process is much more than—and often very different from—a simple effort to replace government processes with markets.

Competitive markets often do not exist for government services. Many of these services (from public assistance to public health and safety) have fuzzy goals that would frustrate full reliance on the markets. The market model often has provided an easy handle with which to grab the reform movement, but its execution has been varied and subtle. Uniting the different efforts are strategies to push operational decisions closer to the front lines; to focus those decisions on results rather than on processes; to increase efficiency by testing government's processes against private markets; to increase the responsiveness of government to its citizens; and to increase the capacity of government, especially central government, to manage effectively.

The Transformation of Public Management

What explains the fact that so many governments pursued such similar strategies so aggressively at much the same time? Four different political-economic forces have been at play:

—*Political:* With the end of the cold war, many nations found themselves amid widespread debates about the role of government. In nations that once lay behind the Iron Curtain, governments had the daunting task of transforming their basic systems of governance, devising institutions that are more democratic, building civil society, and reshaping their relationships with citizens. Developing nations found themselves under quite similar pressures, along with strong calls to modernize their economies quickly. Industrialized nations had to deal with the decline of citizen trust and confidence in public institutions. Candidates around the world have waged successful campaigns on the theme of shrinking government and reducing its work force. Citizens rarely have embraced the idea of a "smaller" government in terms of the services they receive. The political force for somehow shrinking government has nevertheless spread around the world. Together, these forces combined to create strong political pressures for reform.

—*Social:* Some nations faced profound societal transformation. In South Africa, for example, the end of apartheid required the government to find ways to bring disenfranchised blacks into political life. Many Eastern European nations have been working to reconstruct their social, legal, economic, and political systems. In many industrialized nations, standards of living stagnated; many families required two wage earners to match the standard of living that one formerly provided. Finally, societies everywhere struggled to cope with the radical shift from the industrial to the information age. Ideas spread with stunning speed; companies—and nations—that failed to keep up were punished quickly and harshly. These transformations pressed governments strongly toward reform.

—*Economic:* In the late 1990s the Asian flu and other crises brought profound challenges to the financial structure of East Asian nations. After years of "Asian miracles," economic crises brought harsh challenges to the governments and great urgency for reform. Other nations, such as New Zealand and the United Kingdom, launched their reforms to escape economic stagnation and to fuel economic growth. Corporate leaders in many nations have complained that government, especially its tax and regulatory policies, has reduced economic growth and limited their businesses' global competitiveness. Deregulation, privatization, and other tactics to promote job creation and economic growth have been central to the debate.

—*Institutional:* All governments have found themselves part of an increasingly global economy and political system. Major initiatives—military, economic, and political—require careful negotiation and partnership. Within the European Union, nations are racing to harmonize their policies and create supranational structures to shape future programs. Meanwhile, international organizations, including the United Nations, the World Bank, the International Monetary Fund, the Inter-American Development Bank, and the World Trade Organization, are playing big roles in shaping the world community. Nongovernmental organizations have become vastly numerous and very important in shaping political debate and service delivery. Many national governments have devolved power down to the local level. Political power and program administration have simultaneously become more concentrated at levels above the nation-state and less concentrated in subnational governments and civil society. The result is a new constellation of relationships not well understood but hugely important.

Reform and Governance

The reformers have shared their experiences with each other. The reform movement has spread like wildfire, often without careful analysis of the results they have produced or the preconditions for success. In the middle of this wildfire is a profound paradox: Government management is both more and less important than the reform movement suggests.

On one hand, macrogovernance and macroeconomic issues often swamp management reform. What matters most usually is whether the economy is growing and whether citizens think government is working. New Zealanders tend to gauge the success of their nation's reforms by how long they have to wait for medical procedures and how many citizens emigrate to other nations. Swedes assess their reforms by the level of economic growth, continuation of treasured social welfare programs, and maintenance of social cohesion.

On the other hand, government bureaucracy and its management play a central role in these macro-level political and economic issues. For governments to grow, they must manage their debt and public programs effectively. Government managers and elected officials alike have complained that standard bureaucratic procedures frequently handicap their government's ability to respond effectively to global challenges. Hence, government reform is often much more important than it appears on the surface. Without strong public management well-equipped to tackle the problems government faces, governments in many nations have been unable to play their required roles.

In short, as I suggest in this volume, the most important aspect of the global reform movement in public management is that public management is only part of the picture. The problems the movement seeks to solve have to do with government's relationship with civil society. Its strategies and tactics seek to strengthen government's capacity to meet citizens' hopes. The success or failure of the movement depends on how deeply its reforms become wired into a nation's governance systems—its political institutions, public expectations, and civil society.

In fact, the global public management movement is part of a fundamental debate about governance. The implicit assumption is that the government of the past century will not effectively tackle the problems of the next. What should government do? How can it best accomplish those goals? What capacity does it need to do it well? What should be the relationship between the nation-state and multinational organizations? What should be the relationship between nation-states and subnational governments, the private sector, and nongovernmental organizations? How can government best promote democratic accountability? How can the emerging structures and relationships promote the interests of citizens as a whole and escape capture by narrow interests? How can citizen distrust and alienation be minimized? The management reform movement builds on the notion that good governance—a sorting out of mission, role, capacity, and relationships—is a necessary (if insufficient) condition for economic prosperity and social stability.

On the pages that follow I discuss the basic models of reform, especially in New Zealand and the United States. A standard tool kit of strategies and tactics has driven the reforms, in these nations and around the world. They shape important problems of governance and raise profound implications for governance in the twenty-first century.

CHAPTER TWO

Models of Reform

The transformation of governance has produced a reform movement as varied as the world's nations. South Koreans have debated whether there is a distinct Asian cultural and political identity and whether such an identity requires reforms carefully tailored to the region. The Mexican government has launched a twin-edged movement to improve efficiency and reduce corruption. Finland has strengthened its management-by-results system. The Americans have "reinvented," and the United Kingdom has launched multiple attacks on traditional bureaucratic structures. Less developed countries frequently have found themselves whipsawed between pressures to copy the well-known reforms of some developed countries and the need to build basic management capacity. Multinational organizations often have made management reform a precondition for aid, but they have struggled to define which strategies are most likely to be effective.

Global efforts fall roughly into two broad models: Westminster reforms, shaped by the pathbreaking efforts of the New Zealand and the U.K. governments, and American-style reinvention, which was more incremental and, ironically, more sweeping than Westminster-style reform. New Zealand first demonstrated the cutting-edge approach, which has spread to other Westminster-style governments, including Australia and Canada. It defined a "new public management" aimed at shrinking the size of government and imposing a market-style discipline on government. The United States, by contrast, came relatively late to the global movement. Its "reinventing government" strategy produced less fundamental restructuring but more sweeping administrative changes. These two strategies defined the basic models that have powerfully shaped debate around the world.

Managerialism: Westminster-Style Reforms

Modern public management reform had its true start in New Zealand. Indeed, no government has traveled farther or faster in reshaping its public programs or the administrative systems supporting them. The changes not only were enormous but also had an uncommon starting point: They resulted from a carefully thought-out plan of what the reformers wanted to do and how they could accomplish it. The New Zealand reforms began with a top-down approach that sought to privatize programs wherever possible; to substitute market incentives for command-and-control bureaucracies; and to focus single-mindedly on outputs and results instead of inputs, especially budgets. The approach was most remarkable for its universal sweep and aggressive implementation. The reformers attempted nothing less than a complete revolution in what the government did and how it did it, and they fundamentally transformed the very fiber of the New Zealand government. Allen Schick, in the most comprehensive and incisive analysis of the reforms in New Zealand, called it "a singular accomplishment in the development of modern public administration."[2]

The New Zealand government traditionally had been one of the most aggressive in the world in expanding basic rights and government programs.[3] It was the world's first country to grant women the right to vote (in 1893) and later created the world's first "cradle-to-grave" welfare system (in 1935). Its "cocoon economy," as Schick christened it, helped sustain the system.[4] There was little unemployment or inflation, and the standard of living ranked among the world's highest. The economy was highly regulated and subsidized. State-owned enterprises, from transportation and energy to communications, dominated public spending.

By the early 1980s the New Zealand economy could no longer support the nation's ambitious public programs. Faced with tough competition from the emerging Pacific Rim economies and declining agricultural trade with the United Kingdom, the country found itself in economic chaos. The economy stagnated, and inflation soared. Traditional pump-priming strategies failed to stimulate the economy and instead fueled inflation, which led to a run on the New Zealand dollar. The economic crisis cost the National Party its parliamentary majority and brought the Labour Party to power for the first time in nine years.

Heading the Finance Ministry in the new government was Roger Douglas, who pressed for massive changes in government policy and management. Driving those changes was a market-based approach: a commitment to competition, a belief in using market processes to shape the incentives of government employees, and an approach to reform heavily shaped by new institutional economic theories. The approach, quickly christened "Rogernomics," drew first on ideas about transaction costs: The high cost of gathering information about policies strengthens the power of special interests and increases the chance that these interests will capture the attention of decisionmakers. Effective reform requires finding a way for government policymakers to break these connections. It also drew on the theory of the agency problem: Policy management requires policymakers to delegate responsibility to low-level officials through a kind of contract (work delivered in exchange for salary payments). However, effectively supervising these employees is very costly, because it is difficult to define the work clearly, monitor results, and enforce the contracts. Several former New Zealand government officials explained, "The goal for designers of public sector institutions and processes is to avoid public choice problems and minimize agency costs."[5]

The reformers coupled these economic theories with management reform ideas borrowed from the private sector. Corporate managers were preaching that employees could not manage effectively unless they had flexibility to determine the best way to meet policy goals. Douglas and colleagues agreed that managers ought to be held responsible for results. To do so, managers needed freedom to spend within their budgets, to hire the best employees to do the job, and to buy the supplies and equipment they needed for the tasks at hand. Traditional New Zealand administration had given public managers little freedom and imposed heavy controls before the fact. They have sought, in short, to balance two competing approaches: giving managers more flexibility ("letting the managers manage," as they say in New Zealand) while holding them strictly accountable for results ("making the managers manage," the other aphorism puts it).

Two remarkable features characterized this effort. First, powerful theories guided the reforms. Second, these reforms shaped the thinking of officials throughout the government. Douglas and his followers consciously modeled their efforts to deal with the theoretical problems. The formal language of transaction cost economics spread out from the Treasury to government offices throughout Wellington, and soon, high-level discussions about this abstract theory became as common as those about the substance of government programs. The Labour Party government made reform its centerpiece, and its officials launched an ambitious and aggressive campaign to reshape public management.

The New Zealand Strategy

The New Zealand reforms were not so much a single effort but a package that steadily evolved over more than fifteen years of efforts. Indeed, June Pallot has identified four different stages of reform. From 1978 to 1985, the managerialist phase introduced private sector–style management (including accrual accounting) into government operations. The period 1986–91, the marketization phase, brought economic approaches to government management, including contracts, market competition, and individual self-interest. During the strategic phase of 1992–96 the government sought to provide a comprehensive view of government programs to reduce the fragmentation encouraged by marketization. After 1997, in the adaptive capacity phase, the government concentrated on developing the capability to manage the new strategies, especially in human resources.[6]

These reforms have been the world's most aggressive and ambitious. Together, they present a comprehensive and theory-driven package of ideas. The reformers sought first to increase the transparency of government by clearly specifying the goals of government programs and reporting on results. They separated the purchase and production functions. The government would decide what should be done and then rely on whoever could do the job most effectively and cheaply. After elected officials made basic policy decisions, government managers had great discretion over how best to do the job. Cabinet officials—members of the prime minister's government as well as elected parliamentarians—hired chief executives under fixed-term contracts and performance-based incentives to implement programs. The contracts specified outputs (for example, how many miles of roadway to be built or how many children to be vaccinated), held the chief executives responsible for delivering those outputs, and rewarded the chief executives according to how well they accomplished the task.

In general, the reformers tried to separate policymaking from policy administration, replace traditional government bureaucracy and authority with market-driven competition and incentives, make goals and outputs transparent, and give government managers flexibility in determining how to reach these goals. The reforms were not explicitly antigovernmental and did not set out to reshape government operations. Rather, the reformers sought to reduce the scope of government functions, to determine how best to perform them—in government or outside it—and to use results as the ultimate measure of accountability.

PRIVATIZATION AND CORPORATIZATION. The New Zealand government privatized many state-owned, state-run services (including telephone, oil, insurance, post office, and airline companies). In all, the government sold more than twenty state-owned companies.[7] However, the privatization was not nearly as important as a broader effort to increase the productivity of state-owned enterprises. The government viewed these enterprises as entities in which the government held an ownership interest. Its role was to provide the maximum return for taxpayers. The 1986 State-Owned Enterprises Act, which wrote these principles into law, was one of the first and most important pieces of New Zealand reform legislation.

PERFORMANCE CONTRACTING. The 1988 State Sector Act and the 1989 Public Finance Act cemented the reforms in government's core departments. The acts gave chief executives great flexibility in hiring, firing, and paying their employees. The chief executives themselves moved from lifetime tenure to five-year contracts. The New Zealand government made output-based contracts between government officials and government managers the keystone of its reforms.

OUTPUT BUDGETING. The State Sector Act of 1988 made government managers responsible for performance. In particular the act sought to move accountability from inputs (resources used, especially tax dollars) to outputs (the activity—and its quality—produced). The New Zealand reformers have insisted that government managers be held accountable for the results they can control. Many government programs work through administrative intermediaries or depend on social factors for their success. The success of social welfare programs, for example, can depend as much on the performance of the economy (how easy it is to move people from government help to public assistance) as on how well the programs work.

STRATEGIC PLANNING. Since 1992 the New Zealand government has been producing comprehensive accrual budgets. Most governments keep their books on a cash basis (that is, tax dollars collected each year minus government expenditures in the same year). New Zealand became the world's first government to use the accrual method to assess the full cost of its programs, including the long-term cost of commitments already made. Government officials had carefully read the economic theories of government decisionmaking, and they concluded that cash accounting created strong incentives for making decisions today whose full cost would not be borne until much later. Accrual accounting forced them to deal with the full cost of decisions as they made them. Moreover, the Fiscal Responsibility Act of 1994 mandated that the government identify its fiscal objectives and report on how well it achieved them.

The government then mandated the creation of strategic result areas (SRAs) and key result areas (KRAs). Government officials were required to move from broad policy goals to specific strategies that agencies would pursue. These strategies would determine the SRAs on which the agencies would focus over the coming three to five years. The cabinet defined these SRAs, which became binding on the cabinet departments. The SRAs then shaped budget decisions and the specific outputs required of chief executives—the KRAs—in their contracts. The SRAs and KRAs not only shape the budget and accounting systems but also define basic accountability in New Zealand government: who does what, and how the different pieces fit together into governmental policy.

As the government has begun to discuss crosscutting strategies explicitly, government officials have been forced to step back and ponder two related issues. First, the market-driven processes risk atomizing government programs. Government officials are principally responsible for producing the outputs defined in their contracts, not necessarily for how well their programs connect with others. New Zealanders have begun exploring the broader implications of government policy—how outputs cumulate into outcomes. Second, government officials in particular worry about their capacity for taking on the vastly new challenges of managing the reforms. Indeed, Schick pointed out in his seminal study of the New Zealand reforms that these issues represent the puzzles to which the government must next turn as the spirit of reform continues.[8]

Reform the Westminster Way

The New Zealand reforms represent only one of many ambitious movements in countries with British-style parliamentary systems. Australia mounted a similarly strong reform effort. Unlike the New Zealand reforms, which drew heavily on economic theories to transform the incentives of public managers (to "make the managers manage"), the Australian reforms focused on removing barriers to effective administration (to "let the managers manage").[9] The Australians focused on assessing outcomes more than the New Zealanders did. Canada also undertook extensive reforms to shrink the size of government and to improve the coordination of public services.[10]

In the Westminster world the New Zealand reforms remain the most comprehensive and aggressive effort, even though the British reforms are perhaps better known. Whereas the New Zealand reforms were launched from the left, the British reforms grew from the right with Prime Minister Margaret Thatcher's neoconservative venture to shrink the size of the state. In 1982 Thatcher launched the government's Financial Management Initiative. The initiative centered on separating the government's functions into clear responsibility centers, identifying the costs (on an accrual basis) associated with producing outputs in each center, and holding managers strictly accountable for their results. This initiative drew heavily on private sector approaches to production. Later strategies incorporated a heavy customer service component to the production function. British "citizens charters," for example, set service standards for government programs. As part of the Next Steps process, many government bureaucracies were spun off into separate agencies. These new agencies operated under contract to the parent department for the production of specified outputs and in exchange for greater flexibility in using resources. Market testing—privatizing public services where possible and subjecting remaining public services to market competition—aimed to improve the incentives for efficiency.[11]

Together, the British Commonwealth experiments amounted to a "new public management," said analysts. The movement produced a commitment to "managerialism," which Christopher Pollitt called the "seldom-tested assumption that better management will prove an effective solvent for a wide range of economic and social ills."[12] The new public management stemmed from the basic economic argument that government suffered from the defects of monopoly, high transaction costs, and information problems that bred great inefficiencies. By substituting market competition—and marketlike incentives—the reformers believed that they could shrink government's size, reduce its costs, and improve its performance. Sometimes the argument came from the left, as in New Zealand. Sometimes it came from the right, as in the United Kingdom. However, at its core the movement sought to transform how government performed its most basic functions.

Many analysts have questioned whether the new public management is real, whether its underlying market philosophy is valid, and whether it has truly accomplished what it has claimed. Indeed, Laurence E. Lynn Jr. has asked whether the new public management has truly transformed government's core functions. He contends that "there is no new paradigm" shaping theory and practice.[13]

Even if the jury is still out on the long-range impact of the managerial movement, its first two decades nevertheless established clear changes in the Westminster governments. Sandford Borins has identified the following characteristic components: [14]

—*Customer service:* Officials have implemented broad initiatives to improve the responsiveness of public programs.

—*Operating autonomy:* The reforms have separated government functions into quasi-autonomous agencies to give managers more flexibility in pursuing their goals (especially in budget and human resource policies).

—*Output measurement:* Officials have created a results-based measurement system. Both agencies and senior managers work under performance contracts. (However, performance-based pay seems not to have worked.)

—*Human resources:* Downsizing and pay freezes have hurt morale; however, governments are seeking to improve recruitment and training packages to bolster the work force.

—*Information technology:* Its extensive use to improve service delivery has created a new generation of policy issues, from access to privacy, that governments must resolve.

—*Privatization:* Governments have spun off operations to the private sector where possible. They have developed new service delivery partnerships with private and nonprofit organizations.

Although the scholarly debate continues about whether these features represent a new paradigm, there is little doubt that the Westminster reforms have transformed the global debate about governance. These reforms have become the touchstone for all debates about what government does—and how it can do it better.

Reinvention: American-Style Reforms

The American government, by contrast, came to the management reform movement much later than the Westminster governments. Moreover, when the Clinton administration launched the reinventing government campaign in the United States, it was greatly politicized. On one hand, America's sweeping reforms touched more parts of government more quickly than the reforms elsewhere. On the other hand, because of the political conflict it engendered, the reforms focused on changing bureaucrats' behavior rather than transforming the fundamental fiber of government's structure and processes.

After the 1992 presidential election, President Bill Clinton committed the administration to reinventing government—a strategy to make government smarter, cheaper, and more effective. He charged Vice President Al Gore with leading the effort, and Gore devoted singular attention to the job. Reinventing government became the latest step in the American administrative reform movement, one of the true staples of federal politics in the twentieth century.[15]

The Gore effort provoked remarkably different responses. The administration hailed reinvention as "creating a government that works better and cost less."[16] Cynics rejected the effort as meaningless, and critics contended it was dangerous to democracy.[17] Peter Drucker contended that steps Gore claimed as radical were trivial ones that in other institutions "would not even be announced, except perhaps on the bulletin board in the hallway." Drucker said they were the kinds of things "that even a poorly run manufacturer expects supervisors to do on their own—without getting much praise, let alone extra rewards."[18]

Three Faces

Sorting out these claims and complaints is difficult because the Gore-led movement was, in reality, three different reinventions in its first six years—not one. The initiative evolved throughout the Clinton administration, partly to adjust to what the reinventors learned along the way and even more so to respond to lurching political counterpressures.

In Phase I, the administration launched the initiative and scored some important early victories. In Phase II, Clinton reinventors scrambled to cope with the challenges of the Republican takeover of Congress after the 1994 midterm elections. Finally, in Phase III, the reinventors worked to reinvigorate the initiative and to position Gore for the 2000 presidential election. The shifting patterns of reinvention made it difficult to characterize or judge the Clinton administration's reinventing government strategy, but at least they chart the big issues that define it.

PHASE I: WORKS BETTER, COSTS LESS. Gore's effort, christened the National Performance Review (NPR), sent squads of reformers throughout government agencies to identify opportunities for decreasing waste and improving management. For "new Democrats" such as Clinton and Gore, the launch of the reinventing government campaign was a natural first step toward their vision of a new progressivism.[19] "We must reward the people and ideas that work and get rid of those that don't," the Clinton–Gore campaign manifesto had promised.[20] The March 1993 reinventing government announcement put that plan into play. The administration recruited hundreds of federal employees, formed them into teams, and dispatched them throughout the federal bureaucracy. In September 1993 Gore assembled their proposals into a report. In this report he presented 384 recommendations that promised to save $108 billion and to reduce the federal work force by 12 percent within five years.[21]

Although the "works better, costs less" motto had a clever ring to it, it also presented the reinventors with a dilemma.[22] The "works better" approach envisioned motivating and empowering employees to do a better job, whereas the "costs less" aspect sought to eliminate unneeded programs and positions. The reinventors and White House political operatives calculated that their credibility depended on producing large savings. However, producing large savings required tough words and big cuts, especially in the number of government employees, and that strategy made it hard to motivate the employees. The political realities were no easier. Both inside and outside the White House, reinventors felt heavy pressure to show that the NPR was real by reducing the budget. Saving large amounts of money that could officially be counted required reducing federal employment, because this one action could quickly produce substantial savings. The NPR promised to permanently eliminate 252,000 federal employees. Congress later upped the ante to 272,900.

Although downsizing drove the debate, two other initiatives were important in Phase I: procurement reform and customer service. In 1994 Congress passed the Federal Acquisition Streamlining Act. The act simplified procurement regulations and gave managers more flexibility in buying goods off the shelf. It was the first major reform of the government's contracting rules in a decade. It made managers' lives easier and saved hundreds of millions of dollars (although the precise size of the savings was hard to estimate). Reformers soon hailed it as one of the most important accomplishments of the reinventing government program. The administration also mandated that all federal agencies develop customer service plans. Although critics argued that people were citizens or owners, not customers, the customer service initiative undoubtedly launched a major transformation of the way many federal government employees thought about the jobs they did and how they did them. It encouraged government employees to think about the needs of the citizens for whom government programs had been created. For the hundreds of thousands of government employees who focused on helping other government employees get their jobs done, the customer service initiative encouraged them to focus on broader policy goals instead of each agency's narrow self-interest.

Although procurement reform and customer service provided the subtext for Phase I, downsizing remained the defining theme.

PHASE II: WHAT SHOULD GOVERNMENT DO? By the end of 1994 the customer service initiatives were under way, Congress had passed procurement reform, and the administration had significantly downsized the federal work force. Vice President Gore applauded "heroes of reinvention" who had championed better government and cut red tape. Despite its efforts, the Clinton administration watched the Republicans take over both houses of Congress in 1994, for the first time in a generation. The Republicans proceeded to launch a frenzied bidding war to shrink government radically.

The Republican campaign forced the Clinton administration to shift from the Phase I emphasis on how government did its work to what government ought to do. In launching Phase II Gore challenged federal managers to "review everything you do." No program was to be taken for granted. He even asked managers to consider the implications if their agency were eliminated.[24] Quite simply, Gore wanted to counter the Republicans' efforts to challenge what government did and how well it did it.

The Republicans failed to pass most of their proposals. The number of cabinet agencies remained the same, and the threatened massive eradication of federal programs never took place. However, Congress did make substantial budget cuts, and at several points the battle completely closed down the government. In the end the Clinton administration maneuvered its way out of the crisis by outflanking congressional Republicans. Despite the grand rhetorical skirmishes, the battle ended in a draw with little sorting out of government's functions, reorganizing of its operations, or minimizing of its role.

Phase II provided putty for some of the cracks in the political dikes. With his ongoing "hammer awards" (to celebrate breaking through bureaucratic barriers), Gore recognized the work of agency-level reinventors. The customer service movement bore considerable fruit, especially in the Social Security Administration and the U.S. Customs Service. Procurement changes helped make the lives of government managers easier and made the federal government a better partner to its private contractors. The acquisitions work force shrank by one-third, and the Air Force Materiel Command claimed a 64 percent reduction in the number of pages in its acquisitions regulations. Assessing cost savings was difficult; the NPR claims savings of $12.3 billion in the first four years of the effort.[25] However, budgetary battles eroded much of the enthusiasm generated in Phase I and further cemented downsizing and cost saving as the keystones of the NPR.

PHASE III: SEARCH FOR POLITICAL RELEVANCE. In early 1998 Gore shifted the focus of the NPR again. This time, he changed the program name (National Performance Review) to the National Partnership for Reinventing Government ("the NPR with a silent 'G,'" wags suggested). To signal his reinvention of reinvention, Gore gave the new NPR a new slogan: "America @ Its Best." He used the Internet-style motto to emphasize the new role of the information-age government: implementing technologies that could improve its efficiency. He also pledged to continue the quest for better customer service and for broad goals such as building a "safe and healthy America," "safe communities," a "strong economy," and the "best-managed government ever." The administration focused most of its reinvention efforts on thirty-two "high-impact agencies" that dealt most directly with citizens, where the failure to reform quickly could further undermine the effort (as in the case of the Internal Revenue Service [IRS]). For example, the administration committed the Occupational Safety and Health Administration (OSHA) to reducing worker injuries in the 50,000 most dangerous workplaces by 25 percent before the year 2000, the Food and Drug Administration (FDA) to reducing the drug approval process to one year, and the U.S. Postal Service to delivering 92 percent of local first-class mail overnight.[26]

The goal of Phase III, in rhetoric and in reality, was to build an information-age government managed as well as America's best companies. The tactic was to use process reforms to motivate people on the inside and broad policy goals to excite people on the outside.[27] Herein lay the central dilemma of Phase III: Its inside-government game focused on improving the federal government's performance while its outside-government game promised results that the federal government had little role in producing. Federal control over the economy is indirect at best, weak in the short term, and always hard to measure. Local governments police the streets, even if they are aided by extra police funded by federal grants. The health and safety of the nation as a whole is obviously everyone's first concern, but the forces that shape it are so complex that assigning responsibility (or blame or credit, for that matter) is difficult indeed. In seeking political relevance, the reinventors necessarily distanced Phase III of the NPR from its ability to achieve and produce measurable results.

In Phase III the government made promises that it could not directly fulfill. It focused government employees on problems they could not solve themselves. The gap between megapolitics (especially the broad political battles between the administration and Congress) and frontline management (especially the experiments managers tried to improve results) had been a problem during Phases I and II. In Phase III, with more expansive promises and even tougher political battles, the gap threatened to widen even more.

The Impacts of Reinvention

What did the NPR produce? Realism (or, perhaps, cynicism) argues that the NPR did not accomplish all it promised. Pragmatism argues that the goals of the NPR are part of an endless quest never to be completed. The twentieth century alone has seen eleven major government reform initiatives, from the Keep Commission (1905–09) through the two Hoover Commissions (1947–49 and 1953–55) to the NPR.[28] Indeed, as Paul Light has argued, management reform movements have swept American politics in endless "tides of reform."[29] Public management reform never ends.

WORKS BETTER? Energetic administrators throughout the federal government developed imaginative solutions. Managers in radiology departments at Veterans Affairs hospitals developed electronic links that reduced the need for on-call radiologists. Postal workers in Newton, Massachusetts, saved $50 million with a Mover's Guide and a Welcome

Kit that improved service and reduced the Postal Service's costs. The mandate to develop customer service plans had forced all federal agencies to identify and address the customers they were in business to serve, and procurement reform had streamlined the government's buying process. NPR officials claimed that more than 4,000 customer service standards had been implemented in more than 570 government agencies and programs. About 325 "reinvention laboratories" were developing innovative approaches to public service delivery.[30]

However, in many agencies the NPR had little impact. In 1996, more than three years after the launch of the NPR, only 37 percent of federal employees surveyed believed that their organization had made reinvention a top priority. The management improvement goals of the NPR penetrated far less deep into the Pentagon than in civilian agencies.[31] Morale in many agencies was poor. Only 20 percent of federal workers said that the NPR had brought positive change to government. In agencies where the NPR was a top priority, 59 percent of employees thought productivity had improved; where it was not, only 32 percent thought productivity had improved. In agencies where the goals of the NPR had been emphasized, employees were three times as likely to think that government organizations had made good use of their abilities as in agencies where they were not. Employees also were almost twice as likely to believe that they had been given greater flexibility.[32] The attitudes of employees varied with the priority that top managers had placed on reinvention.

The results of that survey underscore one of the most subtle yet most important failures of the NPR effort: Despite Gore's surprising and constant enthusiasm for the initiative, the administration failed to enlist many of its own political appointees in the cause. Without strong political leadership from these appointees, many agencies did not connect with the NPR campaign. Did government work better because of the NPR? Procurement reform and customer service were clear victories, but the wide disparity in reform efforts among agencies made generalized conclusions difficult.

COSTS LESS? What about the NPR's claim that government costs less? The Clinton administration claimed that if all of its recommendations had been adopted, the federal budget would have saved $177 billion by fiscal year 1999. Actual savings, the NPR estimated, totaled $112 billion.[33] However, those claims were unaudited—and unauditable.[34] Some were clear and straightforward: Federal employment was reduced by just over 300,000 positions—15.5 percent, by November 1997—to fewer than 2 million civilian employees.[35] Others were ambiguous and difficult to measure, such as reforms in procurement, information technology, and administrative process. However, no matter how cynical an observer might be, one fact was clear: The NPR did indeed reduce the number of federal government employees to a level lower than any time since the Kennedy administration. Moreover, the reductions in government employment accounted for half of all of the NPR's claimed savings. Even if critics might debate savings estimates on some points, the reinventing government initiative unquestionably saved a substantial amount of money—if only from the documented downsizing.

Where did the downsizing occur? Data indicate that most reductions took place among federal civilian defense employees and low-level federal workers. There is little evidence that it targeted middle and upper management jobs. Overall the federal civilian work force (excluding the U.S. Postal Service) shrank 15.4 percent from January 1993 through April 1998. Defense employment accounted for a large part of the reduction, largely because of the overall reductions of the nation's defense establishment. The procurement work force shrank, as did the number of frontline white- and blue-collar support workers. Employment elsewhere in the bureaucracy shrank less (but reductions varied widely across the government).

In the Pentagon downsizing began before the launch of the NPR. Cynics contended that the NPR simply ratified reductions in the civilian work force at the Department of Defense (DOD) that were going to occur anyway. Some critics argued that the NPR had accomplished little because the Pentagon was already in the process of downsizing, defense employment accounted disproportionately for the NPR's work force reductions, and these work force reductions accounted for the lion's share of the confirmed NPR savings. In fact, the NPR accelerated the defense trend that had already started. It also spread the reductions to the civilian agencies. The reductions were real and, for some government employees, extremely painful. Indeed, if the NPR accomplished nothing else, it certainly produced a substantial and sustained reduction in federal employment—almost across the board— in a way never before seen in the federal government.

In federal departments, the impact of the work force reduction varied widely across the bureaucracy. Although the overall work force was reduced by a little more than one-sixth, the Justice Department actually grew 21 percent (largely because of the hiring of new prison guards) and some agencies and departments were reduced only slightly. The Environmental Protection Agency (EPA), for example, shrank 2.2 percent and the Department of Health and Human Services 4.2 percent. Other agencies took much bigger hits: The Department of Housing and Urban Development downsized by 23.1 percent, the Department of Defense by 23.4 percent, the General Services Administration by 30.8 percent, and the Office of Personnel Management (OPM) by 47.4 percent.[36] The OPM spun off most of the governmental personnel decisions into the agencies, whereas Department of Defense reductions were part of a far larger downsizing of the military. The federal government's downsizing was not one phenomenon but many; the reasons were as varied as the agencies themselves.

The Clinton administration also had committed itself to a reduction in the federal government's middle management. This part of the strategy mirrored the private sector reforms of the 1980s, in which "delayering" and other tactics to reduce the distance from top managers to frontline workers dominated corporate transformations. The argument, in both cases, was simple. Top-level managers make the key policy decisions; frontline workers deliver the services. However, mid-level managers, the argument went, pushed paper and contributed to bureaucracy. Reformers believed that minimizing the number of bureaucratic layers and increasing the span of control (that is, the number of employees each manager supervised) would better focus organizations on their work and improve their responsiveness to customers.

This rhetoric drove the federal government's downsizing. However, the results were very different. The biggest reductions in the federal government's employment came not in the management ranks but in support positions. Workers in the government's general schedule (GS) levels 1–4 (low-level clerical and blue-collar workers) shrank by about half. The number of mid-level clerical workers (GS 5–8) as well as entry- and mid-level professional and technical workers (GS 9–12) decreased. However, the number of managers (GS 13–15) actually increased a bit. Quite simply, the reality did not match the rhetoric.[37]

What accounts for this disparity? Almost all personnel reductions were voluntary. The government made available $25,000 payments, in addition to accrued retirement benefits, for workers who agreed to leave the government. It meant that the fit between the NPR's overall downsizing strategy and its long-term results depended far more on individuals' calculations than on the decisions of the NPR's chiefs. Even more important, the reductions depended on shifts in the federal government's management and policy strategies. Much of the reduction in GS 1–4 came through defense downsizing. As military bases closed, the workers most likely affected were blue-collar support staff, from mechanics to janitors. These workers tended to fall near the bottom of the federal government's pay system and, for the most part, moved to employment in the private sector. In addition, the federal government markedly increased its contracting out for services ranging from cafeterias in federal buildings to planning for government programs. This strategy was fueled by reductions in the GS 5–12 employees who previously might have done this work and by the overall strategy of reducing government employment where possible. More contracting out meant proportionately fewer frontline workers (because the front lines were increasing in the private sector under contract) and proportionately more high-level managers (who were charged with negotiating, writing, and overseeing the contracts). Thus much of the NPR's downsizing reflects not so much the "reduce middle management" rhetoric as the shifting tactics of federal program implementation.

Indeed, the decrease in the number of low-level federal workers while the number of high-level workers remained constant, or even increased, is part of a longer term "grade creep." During the past thirty years, the average grade level of federal employees has been inching upward, from about a GS 7 in 1960 to more than GS 9 at the turn of the century. Critics occasionally have pointed to grade creep as evidence of the federal government's increasing bureaucracy and self-absorption. Part of the source is undoubtedly the increase in the federal government's layers. Paul Light has concluded that the federal government has accumulated layers, especially at top levels of the bureaucracy, that have reduced the federal government's responsiveness and impeded its effectiveness.[38]

Much of the grade creep flows directly from the federal government's changing policy tactics. As federal entitlement, grant, loan, and regulatory programs have increased—and direct service delivery has steadily decreased—the federal work force has adjusted accordingly. A government that delivers few services directly and relies on private contractors, state and local governments, and nonprofit organizations to do the job instead will naturally have fewer low-level workers and proportionately more high-level managers.

The more complex question is whether the NPR accelerated the well-established trend. Evidence indicates that the downsizing and changes in administrative tactics that the NPR represented may have further shifted

government employment to top-level workers. What is difficult to separate out is the contribution of defense downsizing to this trend. The
defense buildup of the 1980s tended to lower the grade level of federal
workers, as the Pentagon added clerical staff to process contracts and
defense workers in the field. Defense downsizing naturally would have
reduced this trend and, as it reduced lower level employees, driven the
average grade level back up. Only time will show the NPR's contribution
to the federal government's grade creep. However, in the long run the
NPR appears to have modestly accelerated a well-established trend based
in the federal government's changing strategies and tactics.

The NPR is most notable for its failure to grapple with these long-run
trends. Its top officials preached the virtues of reducing middle management just as the private sector was rediscovering the importance of middle managers as "high-impact players."[39] The NPR failed to deal with the
layering of government and especially with the 3,000 political appointees
that encrust the top of the federal bureaucracy, for the obvious political
reasons. Coupled with the NPR's failure to enlist those appointees aggressively in its cause, that oversight marked a major shortcoming of the program. It also made it harder for the NPR to deliver on its promise to
downsize middle-level management en route to better customer service. It
is hard to reduce the distance from top managers to the shop floor when
the shop floor—those who actually deliver the government's goods and
services—increasingly lies outside the government.

Did the government cost less as a result of the NPR? Although the
NPR unquestionably decreased costs, especially through procurement
reform and fewer government employees, assessing which of the recommendations produced which savings is a virtually impossible task for two
reasons: because it usually was difficult to predict what costs would have
been without the NPR and because the government's cost accounting systems frequently make such analyses impossible.

The one certain conclusion is that the federal civilian work force was
smaller than it would have been without the NPR, and that this reduction has saved substantial salary and benefit costs, in both the short
term and the long term. It also is likely that the grade creep in the per-
manent work force accelerated. Other savings (for example, in areas
such as procurement reform) are real but more difficult to assess
because we do not know what the government's costs would have been
absent the reforms. Finally, many claimed savings are hopes and wishes

whose value cannot be determined. Did the NPR produce real savings? Yes, specifically, in downsizing the federal work force and in streamlining procurement.

THE FRUITS OF REINVENTION. Whatever its economic and programmatic impact, the NPR has one clear political result: It inescapably connected Vice President Al Gore, who tirelessly led the effort, with management reform. In fact, many political observers surprisingly noted Gore's consistent and energetic pursuit of reinvention, despite its obvious lack of political sex appeal and the many other demands on his time as one of the Clinton administration's few proven "go-to" officials. As the vice president geared up his 2000 presidential campaign, the NPR had become part of his identity, along with environmental policy and high tech initiatives. Gore sensed the importance of the NPR but became entrapped in its political paradox. Bruising battles over health care reform, Social Security, and Medicare showed how little stomach Americans had for major policy initiatives—and how much they wanted a government that worked better.

The Clinton administration promised a government closer to the people (smaller, more effective, with better customer service), but the effort—clearly designed for its political potential in luring Perot voters and defining a "new Democrat" approach to governance in 1993—barely registered on the political radar screen. It often was buried under the avalanche of stories about political fundraising and Whitewater. Reports of taxpayer abuse at the IRS, from armed agents bursting into taxpayers' homes to complaints about indecipherable tax instruction, further undermined the effort. The IRS scandals were precisely the kind of government problems that the NPR was designed to root out. They put Gore and the NPR in a difficult situation. The NPR, designed as a signature Clinton administration initiative, had failed to ignite popular enthusiasm. Focused on improving government performance, it had failed to insulate the administration from major embarrassment. Conceived as an administrative strategy to provide political support, reinvention had significant but uneven administrative results and relatively little political impact.

Nevertheless, the federal government's productivity challenge—getting more government service from less taxpayer money—made reinvention inescapable and continued reform inevitable. In the process, the reinventors worked to devise new strategies to provide extra control over the government's activities.

THE GOVERNMENT PERFORMANCE AND RESULTS ACT. Passed in 1993, GPRA required all federal agencies to set strategic plans for their activities and indicators for measuring their outcomes by March 2000. Previous federal reformers had launched a parade of similar, if less ambitious, efforts: Defense Secretary Robert McNamara's only partly fulfilled promise in the 1960s to bring a planning, programming, and budgeting system (PPB) to the Pentagon; Richard Nixon's goal and objective–based system, management by objectives (MBO); Jimmy Carter's effort to promote zero-based budgeting (ZBB); and organizational behavior reforms in the 1980s through total quality management (TQM). The alphabet of reforms—PPB begot MBO, which begot ZBB, which begot TQM—led to GPRA. Cynics quickly predicted that the ambitious new search for federal goals and outcomes soon would lead to the employment of many consultants and yet another acronym to replace a failed strategy. Some government managers, cynical from the constant parade, concluded that they could safely burrow in and allow this new reform to pass them by.

GPRA was different from previous efforts in two significant ways. First, Congress invested itself directly in GPRA by passing it into law. Second, both Congress and the Clinton administration quickly found political value in the legislation. In 1997 House Majority Leader Dick Armey discovered that GPRA provided a device for bringing executive branch officials before congressional committees to answer for their programs. His GPRA "report cards" attracted media attention and embarrassed many senior federal managers. The Office of Management and Budget (OMB), for its part, began relying on GPRA to shape agencies' activities. As entitlements and other uncontrollable spending took up a steadily rising share of the federal budget, OMB officials were eager for a tool that improved their control of the operations of federal agencies. These political incentives produced big political squabbles but also gave the GPRA a bigger spotlight than its predecessors ever enjoyed. Third, some agencies, including EPA, the National Aeronautics and Space Administration (NASA), IRS, and the Department of Defense, began using the GPRA process to improve internal management. Even though the applications have been rudimentary, GPRA will achieve greater staying power to the degree that GPRA proves useful to managers in improving the way they manage their agencies. Indeed, the principal weakness of its predecessors was the failure of the reform tools to become integrated with internal management—and external political—processes.

INFORMATION TECHNOLOGY. Vice President Gore has become at least as well-known for his interest in the Internet and technology as he is for his interest in reinventing government. Indeed, for the Clinton reinventors, the NPR and information technology are inextricable. They see information technology as the central nervous system for the government of the future: a way to make tax filing easier, to make services more integrated, to make customer service better. In fact, when the administration launched Phase III of the NPR in the spring of 1998, the information-based "office of the future" was one of its signature pieces.

Throughout 1999 the information technology leadership of NPR was more rhetorical than real, primarily because the NPR had a tiny staff and because the structure of the federal government is extraordinarily complex. However, the reformers' instinct to focus on information technology offers great potential. The less hierarchy shapes public management, the more managers need tools to cross bureaucratic boundaries and to link interdependent operations. Moreover, reformers everywhere have sought to improve the integration of public services—for example, to bring together the job training, day care, transportation, and job placement services on which welfare reform depends. Service integration means thinking spatially instead of functionally: from the bottom up, about how programs come together to affect service recipients, instead of from the top down, as top managers and policymakers create and shape individual programs.[40]

DEVOLUTION. While Gore worked to reinvent the federal government, a subtle revolution quietly transformed American management. The federal government increasingly devolved administrative responsibilities and policy-shaping decisionmaking to the states. Americans had invented modern federalism in the eighteenth century, and the states always have had substantial responsibility for many domestic programs. However, in the twentieth century the federal government expanded the scope of domestic policy and imposed new restrictions on the states in managing them. As the federal government struggled to reinvent its own operations, it passed more responsibility back to the states.

For example, the federal government proudly "ended welfare as we know it" by giving the states responsibility for getting welfare recipients off the dole and into productive jobs. EPA delegated more authority to the states in devising strategies for reaching pollution reduction goals. The states experimented with new managed care plans for their Medicaid recipients and devised innovative performance management systems.

Moreover, the states vastly expanded their reliance on private and non-profit contractors in programs ranging from welfare to prisons as they struggled to make their operations cheaper and more effective.

The connection between administrative reform and political results has been tight at the state and local levels. The evidence from America's states and cities supports this conclusion. A new generation of pragmatists has risen to many state capitals and city halls. In the nation's best-run states and cities, it is hard to find a distinctly Republican or Democratic theme that shapes the new approach to policy problems. From Republican mayor Stephen Goldsmith's massive privatization of Indianapolis public services to Democratic mayor Michael White's transformation of Cleveland, a new generation of state and local officials has defined success by getting things done. These efforts do not indicate that the political parties have evaporated or that Mayor Rudolph Giuliani no longer trumpets his Republicanism as the reason for the reduction of New York's crime. However, it does mean that state and local elected officials—especially the most successful ones—have made getting results their number-one priority. Voters, in turn, have looked to results more than party in casting their ballots. The triumph of pragmatism over partisanship has produced widely heralded successes (cheaper, more effective, more responsive government) as well as clear political payoffs, because voters elect leaders with demonstrated track records.

Indeed, one of the great ironies of the effort to reinvent and shrink the federal government is that it promoted the transfer of more programs to the states. This devolution clearly has improved the responsiveness of American government, but it has blurred the lines of responsibility and made it harder to determine who is accountable for which results. American devolution is a triumph of pragmatism but also an often bewildering sharing of administrative power. Especially compared with reforms in other nations, which sought to set sharp policy goals and then establish clear responsibility for results, the American reforms have blurred the process of setting and achieving goals. They also have made the process of determining exactly who is responsible for which results more difficult. Management reform in the U.S. government has a unique style, very different from efforts elsewhere in the world.

Reinvention's Lessons

Even though the Clinton administration's reinventing government initiative encountered serious problems, it showed genuine accomplishment in its first five years. It saved a significant amount of money, brought substantial managerial reforms (especially in customer service and procurement processes), and promoted a more performance-based discussion about the functions of government. Vice President Gore so strongly championed the campaign that Republicans determined to tar him with its shortcomings.

However, the shortcomings of the NPR are as instructive as its early successes. President Clinton's bold proclamation about the end of "big government" missed the far more important if much more subtle transformation in the way government works in the United States. The NPR demonstrated, in its achievements and its failures, that the federal government is no longer organized for the job that law and the Constitution charge it to do. The federal government particularly has not built the capacity required to effectively manage a government increasingly operated through proxies. Both Democrats and Republicans have been politically burned on megapolicy initiatives, and neither side has shown much stomach for further adventures.

For these reasons the management agenda is all the more important. They also underline an important point: that management reform is at least as much about politics and governance as it is about management. Beyond this point is a more subtle one: Policy initiatives have important management implications that can be ignored only at great political peril.

CHAPTER THREE

Strategies and Tactics

The global government reform movement has focused on two problems. One problem is policy, with roots in politics: What should government do? Can—or should—government be smaller? The policy questions revolve around value problems and depend on the political process to sort them out. The other problem is administration, with roots in efficiency and effectiveness: How can government do what it does better? Can we do more with less and, in the process, improve the satisfaction of citizens? The administrative questions revolve around management reform and depend on improving the management process—especially traditional bureaucratic authority.

The global reform debate includes several different answers to these questions. One New Zealander is fond of pointing out that his mother, when asked her opinion of the government's administrative reforms there, replies that it still takes six months to get a gall bladder operation. Citizens, and many elected officials, often fail to distinguish between deciding what to do and determining how to do it better. Of course, often there is no practical distinction between such political and administrative issues. Government is what government does. Government reform hinges on deciding which of these processes to change to improve what government does.

The global administrative reform tactics share a common approach: trying to remedy a pathology of traditional bureaucracy that is hierarchically structured and authority-driven. In many ways bureaucracy has proven itself a noble invention. In both the private and public sectors, it has allowed humans to coordinate complex activities in efficient ways. However, critics of bureaucracy have contended that bureaucracy—especially public bureaucracy—also has produced a host of problems. Bureaucracies can become locked into "iron triangles" and tight "issue networks," in which interest groups and narrow legislative pressures can distort administration. According to the critics, bureaucracies produce miles of red tape.[41] They can become inflexible and rude. They can become consumed by incentives to maximize their own power at the expense of public goals.[42] The complaints about bureaucracy have spread quickly and globally, to that point that "bureaucracy" is a dirty word the world over.

As a central part of their efforts, reformers have sought to transform bureaucracy and the incentives that drive it. The Australians, for example, have viewed bureaucrats as good people trapped in bad systems. They have worked to sweep away impediments to "let the managers manage." The New Zealanders, by contrast, have viewed bureaucrats as utility maximizers. They have worked to transform the incentives of bureaucrats to "make the managers manage."[43] Whatever the approach, the global reform movement has built on a singular effort to transform public bureaucracy.

Herein lies the central dilemma for reformers. Despite its pathologies, bureaucracy is an essential tool of modern government. How can its essential elements be preserved while transforming its behavior? What does government need to do to support the effort?

Reform: Governance and Management

One lesson comes through clearly from the assessment of the management reform strategies: These strategies are as much about politics as administration. Indeed, basic governance issues shape the management options. In addition, though, fundamental and common management problems shape the reform strategies.

Governance

If the Westminster and American reforms are the basic models of reform, then the variation between the models defines the basic issues of reform. The American reforms rank among the most sweeping. Reinventing government sought to transform the entire U.S. federal government in a very short time—to focus government on the customer, improve its effectiveness, and decrease its costs. GPRA catapulted the federal government past fifteen years of Westminster experimentation with output measures to a quick, aggressive move into outcome assessment. However, despite contentious debates about what government ought to do, officials from both parties found the question too hot to handle. Six years of reinvention left the federal government about the same size in scope and scale. It had fewer employees, but it also had devolved many responsibilities to state and local governments and to private and non-profit contractors who did much of the federal government's work.[44] In the end the NPR sought to make the existing government work better and cost less. The complexity of American government—especially the separation-of-powers system and the divided parties within it—make it impossible to achieve consensus on what government ought to do. It left the Clinton administration's reinventors to focus on administrative remedies that avoided basic policy choices.

Therefore, in the global management reform movement, the basic strategies have been shaped partly by scale (how governments have attempted to reshape their basic package of services fundamentally) and partly by the degree of difficulty (how hard it is to build consensus with a nation's governance system about that package of services). The management reform movement is about government administration—its structures, tools, and processes. However, administration is inextricably linked to governance, and both are rooted in politics. The first generation of reforms teaches an important lesson: The strategies of management reform must fit into a nation's governance system—and they must be supported by the political system for the administrative reforms to succeed.

These basic strategies also vary on tactical dimensions (table 3-1). The Westminster reformers have relied heavily on privatization and other market-type mechanisms. They have focused heavily on outputs but only modestly on traditional bureaucratic reorganization. The United States privatized little—the federal government had few state-owned enterprises such as telephone companies and airlines to sell off—so it relied much on public–private partnerships and contracting. Its separation-of-powers system encouraged substantial decentralization to lower levels of the bureaucracy in issues ranging from personnel policy to customer service. Meanwhile its federal system led to more devolution in areas that ranged from welfare reform to environmental policy. The Nordic countries presented a hybrid approach and relied modestly on market mechanisms but much more on reorganization and budgetary reforms.

The basic strategies not only varied by kind of government and degree of change in government's role but also varied significantly but subtly in the tactics the nations used. The tactics were partly the product of the options that each nation's governance system permitted and encouraged. They were the products of what each nation sought to accomplish. They were the products of substantial cross-fertilization. Indeed, one of the most significant features of the global revolution in public management is the spread of reform ideas. Reformers often have been tempted to pluck ideas out of context—for example, from New Zealand's contract-based output system to American welfare reform—and without assessing the links with the governance system that created them. One of the most important lessons of management reform strategies is that they must fit with and be supported by the governance systems in which they are located.

Management

In most countries the management reform movement has sought to root out traditional bureaucracy and the pathologies that reformers believed flowed from it. They tried to root out authority-driven hierarchical systems. They sought to replace them with more competition (driven by market strategies) and responsiveness (driven by a stronger attention to citizens as customers). This approach has brought three fundamental issues to the surface.

First, the reform strategies do not manage themselves. They require energetic management by highly skilled public managers. However, few of the reforms have been purely market-driven. Privatization, for example, relies on shifting public programs to the private market, but it can happen only once. After state-owned enterprises (telephone and other utilities, airlines, postal services) are sold off, government is left with the job of managing what remains. Experience demonstrates quite clearly that tactics such as outsourcing, customer service, and information technology do not—and cannot—manage themselves. Indeed, they require aggressive and thoughtful oversight.

Second, such oversight requires a substantially different capacity than traditional government tools managed through traditional bureaucracies.[45] Contracts, vouchers, tax incentives, loan programs, and other indirect tools of government differ from direct service delivery through bureaucracies in two ways:

—Although government might purchase the service, it does not directly provide it. Rather, proxies (in the private or nonprofit sectors, or

Table 3-1. *Dimensions of Public Management Reforms by Type, 1980–96*

Reform strategy	Westminster		Nordic			American
	United Kingdom	New Zealand	Denmark	Sweden	Finland	United States
Privatization	High	High	Low	Low	Low	Low[a]
Use of market-type mechanisms	High	High	Low	Medium	Medium	Low
Decentralization	Medium	Medium	Medium	Medium–high	Medium	High
Output orientation	High	High	Medium	Medium	High	Low
Traditional restructuring	Low	Low	Medium	High	High	Medium
Intensity of implementation process	Medium–high	High	Low	Medium–low	Medium–low	Medium

Sources: Derived from Christopher Pollitt and others, *Trajectories and Options: An International Perspective on the Implementation of Finnish Public Management Reforms* (Helsinki: Ministry of Finance, 1997); Swedish Agency for Administrative Development, in Statskontoret, *The Swedish Central Government in Transition* (Stockholm, 1998), p. 80; and the author's analysis of the U.S. federal government.

a. Levels of contracting out are very high.

in other levels of government) produce the service instead. In the United States, for example, nearly ninety cents of every federal dollar is spent through proxies and entitlements—individuals, state and local governments, and private and nonprofit contractors who manage programs on behalf of the federal government.[46] How well these programs work depends on how well the government's proxies manage the programs on the government's behalf.

—Only a very small part of the federal budget even remotely matches the traditional hierarchically structured, authority-based governance model. Government managers operate in bureaucracies, organized hierarchically and controlled by authority, to manage tools that increasingly operate by neither hierarchy nor authority. This is not a purely American phenomenon. The Paris-based Organization for Economic Cooperation and Development (OECD) has invested substantial energy in understanding forms of "alternative service delivery."[47]

Third, the global reform movement seeks to strengthen government's ability to develop coordinated responses to problems that stretch beyond the boundaries of individual bureaucracies. American reinventors sought "one-stop shopping,"[48] whereas the Canadian government explored "citizen-centered program delivery."[49] A 1999 British government white paper committed the government to "joined-up government"—one-stop shops to improve the coordination of government services. The government created new offices and also expanded "virtual" coordination through telephone and Internet information services. In fact, the British government experimented with organizing services around major life events—births, start of school, marriage, death—with government organizations joining together to make these transitions easier.[50] The Scottish government, with powers newly devolved from London, considered "the possible Scot," a strategy for joined-up government that pulled together related health care services.[51]

Reform Tactics: Transforming the Bureaucracy

Bureaucracy's greatest strength lies in coordinating complex operations. However, bureaucracy in the twenty-first century raises a host of new coordination problems, because no bureaucracy can completely encompass, manage, or control any problem that really matters.

Harold Seidman has pointed out that coordination is the "philosopher's stone" of public management. Medieval alchemists believed that if they could find the magic stone, they would find the answers to human problems. Coordination, Seidman argues, has the same appeal for managers and reformers. "If only we can find the right formula for coordination," he wrote, "we can reconcile the irreconcilable, harmonize competing and wholly divergent interests, overcome irrationalities in our government structures, and make hard policy choices to which no one will disagree."[52] Coordination becomes the answer to government's problems and the diagnosis of its failures.

Administration, in both public and private life, is a search for social coordination. It is how leaders pull together widely disparate resources— money, people, expertise, and technology—to get complex things done. The implementation of public programs is an intricate dance, whether it is the dispatch of highly trained firefighters to the scene of a blaze or the high-tech ballet that allows planes to operate safely in the air traffic control system. The global management reform movement is partly about better fitting government's programs to citizens' wants, but it also is about building new tools to improve the coordination among governmental programs.

Budgeting and Accounting

The New Zealand reforms laid the foundation for changes in budgeting and accounting tactics. Its output-driven accrual accounting system provided the foundation for reforms in many other nations, especially in the Westminster countries. The Nordic countries joined with New Zealand in top-down, fiscally driven budget policy in which the government set broad policy targets and set agency budgets accordingly. Although most other countries did not follow their lead in top-to-bottom reform, some nations substantially increased managers' flexibility in deciding how to meet their targets within a broad allocation. In Canada's Expenditure Management System, for example, managers fund new initiatives by reallocating their existing budgets.[53] "Portfolio budgeting" in Australia and the Nordic countries give managers discretion in how to meet mandated savings targets. In Australia, Denmark, and Sweden, managers enjoy "efficiency dividends": They are allowed to keep some of the savings they produce.[54]

Accrual accounting, especially in the Westminster countries, has been an important tool in making government more transparent. Reformers have tried to force government officials to confront the full cost of their decisions as they make them, rather than to rely on short-term accounting devices to shift the costs of present decisions to future years. Most other nations, including the United States, stayed with cash-based accounting systems (in which each year's budget is a snapshot of the balance between income and expenses).

In most nations, reformers have looked to budgeting and accounting systems as the very foundation of their efforts. Money provides the most crucial input for most government programs. Tracking the money provides the most useful indicator of activity. Reshaping the flow of money provides perhaps the most useful incentive for changing managers' behavior. Hence budgeting and financial management are the bedrock on which most other reforms have been built.

Performance Management

Reformers have transformed performance measurement into performance management by linking the assessment process with management of government's strategies and tactics. New Zealand's agency-based contracts, which tie together the government's goals, the agency's budget, and program outputs, are the prototype, but other governments have imitated the approach. The United Kingdom has used a similar approach, and the United States has moved aggressively in an effort to couple strategic plans with outcomes.

Many governments have extended program-based performance measures to people-based assessments—performance pay systems for government managers. These systems have spread to Australia, Ireland, the United Kingdom, the United States, and Denmark. However, an OECD survey of government workers in five nations found that performance-driven pay was a relatively weak motivator for their work. In fact, it ranked last of fourteen different factors in the survey. The report concluded that independence on the job, a sense of accomplishment, and having challenging work were far more important motivators.[55] Managers worried that they could not fully understand the criteria by which they were being judged and that the money available for performance pay often did not match their performance awards. In general, managers did not object to the concept of performance-driven pay, but they did not believe that awards were distributed fairly or predictably.[56] Other studies have produced remarkably uniform conclusions.[57]

The managerialist movement, founded in economic theories of bureaucracy that presume incentives motivate performance, had suggested that performance-driven pay would reshape the behavior of government managers. However, in practice the performance-driven pay systems have tended not to be funded or implemented predictably. Senior government managers in particular have paid far more attention to the challenges their jobs offered. Put differently, public managers around the world have indeed been strongly motivated by incentives, but the incentives have had more to do with their jobs than with the often sporadic performance-driven pay systems. The OECD study concluded that there were serious questions about "whether [performance-related pay] awards of any form or size will ever have sufficient value for public sector managers" to make the tactic effective.[58]

The New Zealand and U.K. experience had proven the value of measuring the outputs of public programs. Indeed, such performance management systems became the keystone of reform efforts around the world. In the United States, discussion began on using performance measures to find balance among competing customers' expectations and vice versa. This system has led to "families" of performance measures that allow managers to assess the impacts of their programs on different groups.[59] However, extensions of the tactic—both from outputs to outcomes and from programs to managers—had proven troublesome. Only more experience will tell whether the problems stem from a lack of experience or from inherent limitations of the tools.

Contracting

Reformers have relied extensively on expanded partnerships with nongovernmental organizations (contractors in the private and nonprofit sectors). In nations with federal systems—especially Australia, Canada, and the United States—reformers also have substantially expanded partnerships between the national and state governments. The reasons are both political and administrative. Nations everywhere have faced strong citizen demands to shrink the size of the state. Such partnerships provide ways of getting government's work done without government itself having to do it. Moreover, partnerships provide governments with more flexibility for tackling tough management chores. They often can hire and fire partners far more easily than they can shift the number of government workers, and through such partnerships they can often acquire much-needed skills more easily than recruiting and training their own workers.

Perhaps most important, much of the contracting movement has been driven by an assumption that government is inherently inefficient and that by relying more on nongovernmental contractors, government can reduce its costs and improve its results. Some of this assumption is a powerful ideological belief from the right, often quite untested by evidence, about the presumed superiority of the private sector. More subtly, some of it flows from a belief that government's role is primarily to define its goals and that it does not necessarily have to produce services itself. The former argument has dominated debate in the United States, where privatization, contracting, and other forms of shifting power from government to the private sector have come largely from conservative circles.[60] The latter argument, by contrast, dominated thinking in the Westminster countries, especially New Zealand.

This disparity in the underlying philosophy has led to very different public–private partnerships around the world. In the United States the presumed superiority of the private sector has led some reformers, especially at the state and local level, to contract out everything possible. They assumed that simply shifting the administrative tool to contracting would improve efficiency naturally. Also in the United States this presumed superiority has led to relatively less concern about how best to structure and manage partnerships; simply creating them, some reformers assumed, would lead to better results. In New Zealand a different kind of antibureaucratic ideology drove the debate. Reformers assumed that self-interested incentives of bureaucrats crippled their performance and that a contract-based system between purchasers of government services (the government and its cabinet) and their providers (in the bureaucracy or in nongovernmental partners) would prevent these difficulties. This assumption increased attention on the need to manage contracts well, because the principal agent economic theory that supported the movement also worried extensively about pathologies of contracts, especially transaction costs (such as information and supervision problems). Moreover, there was no built-in bias toward contracting out of government. The job was to be done by whoever could do it best.

The evidence for these theories remains rather thin. Far more decisions have been based on ideology than on research. Nevertheless, a 1998 OECD survey of experiences in Australia, Denmark, Iceland, Sweden, the United Kingdom, and the United States showed that savings from contracting out ranged from 5 to 50 percent; typical savings reported in the study were 20 percent.[61] However, the "level playing field" argument always intrudes on these measures: Do contractors provide service at the same level as government workers? Do they maintain the same focus on broad social values, such as fairness and equality? Do they bid low at the beginning to get the contract and then raise prices later? Although the OECD report acknowledged, "There is some debate whether levels of quality of service were always maintained while these savings were being achieved," it nevertheless concluded, "What does seem clear is that effectively implemented contracting out can lead to productivity improvements."[62]

The key issue, at least in the Australian and in some American experience, is the existence of real competition (or what the Australians call contestability). It is not so much the publicness or privateness of an activity that determines its efficiency but, as one OECD study found, "the *prospect* of competition" that is most likely to improve efficiency and effectiveness. The study concluded, "Contestability in the public service does not necessarily imply transfer or provision of services to the private sector. In numerous instances [in Australia], services that were once provided by the Federal public service are now being delivered by a different arm or level of government. Indeed, many services continue to be delivered by the same provider but in a better manner because of the effect of contestability."[63]

The Australian study found that contestability provided substantial savings. The Defence Commercial Support Program, for example, achieved recurring annual savings of AUS$100 million, and Australia Post increased annual productivity growth from 1 percent in 1990 to 6.8 percent in 1993–94. Contestability also improved service and product quality, transparency, and accountability.[64]

Similarly, in the United States competition between public and private suppliers of public services has underlined the value of contestability. Since 1979 Phoenix has put up for bid fifty-six different service decisions in thirteen different functional areas, ranging from data entry and fuel distribution to street sweeping and senior citizen housing management. In thirty-four cases private contractors submitted the low bids. However, in twenty-two competitions city workers won the work—and outcompeted private bidders. In the process, the city saved $27 million.[65] In Indianapolis local officials moved aggressively to a process they called "contracting in."[66] It proved to be the process of competition, not who won such competitions, that provided the efficiency gains.

The key to making such processes work is capacity within government to write and manage contracts effectively. Government, in short, must become a smart buyer; it must clearly specify what it wants to buy, run fair and competitive markets, and carefully assess the quality of what it buys.[67] The need for effective contract management has led to the development of new management tools.[68]

In the United States the NPR's procurement reforms played a major role in reinvention, and Vice President Al Gore has emphasized the role of common sense in government procurement. The U.S. Navy, for example, had procurement regulations that called for "ruggedized" telephones on board its ships. These devices, which were guaranteed to continue working even if the ship sank, cost $450 per unit. In the new aircraft carrier U.S.S. *John C. Stennis*, the procurement officers installed instead new off-the-shelf phones that cost $30 each. Gore admitted, laughing, "If the ship sinks and is refloated, this phone will not work." He added, "If you do the calculation, you would actually have to sink and refloat the ship fifteen times in order to enjoy the cost savings from the ruggedized phone. So, we've decided to just buy these phones at commercial outlets instead of the specialized. And you know, if your ship is sinking and being refloated fifteen times, you're going to be worried about other things than telephone calls anyway."[69]

Customer Service

The concept of improving government's service to citizens—and using this strategy to transform bureaucracy—has been one of the most robust features of reform. It is a two-part effort. To improve citizens' trust in and support for government, public officials have worked to make government services friendly, convenient, and seamless. Instead of making citizens accommodate themselves to government—its schedules and its way of doing business—officials have tried to accommodate government to citizens.

An NPR report argued, "We have to restore confidence that we can all work effectively together through self-government. And the government has to build confidence just like Ford—or any good company—does. With each and every customer." Government "was getting away from us," the report continued. "It was marching to different drummers—special interests, Washington professionals, well-meaning people with good intentions—on a path that seemed to be headed away from the taxpaying customers of government." By developing customer service strategies that focus on what people want, the report concluded, government could map out "a dramatic change of direction, a big U-turn, to head government back to the people."[70] Customer service, the NPR believed, would both help restore confidence in government and provide a powerful engine for changing how government does its job. In fact, the Social Security Administration surprised the business world when an independent survey found the agency had the country's best toll-free telephone service.[71]

The movement toward better customer service has been very broad. In addition to the United Kingdom's "citizens charters," Belgium, France, and Portugal have set standards for customer service. In Australia, France, and Germany, citizens can receive written explanations of government decisions that affect them.[72] Many governments, both national and local, have developed "whole of client," "one-stop shopping," interactive technology, or case management strategies to make service delivery more seamless for citizens. Italy, for example, has established a one-stop shop for businesses where a single office can provide authorization for the location and startup of a new plant or the expansion of an existing one.[73] The French government has even used the services of a "qualitician" to expand customer service concepts.[74] In South Africa tactics to increase the transparency of government and improve its customer service were central to the government's efforts to uproot apartheid. The national *Bitupili* ("people first") program established measurable outcomes, public reporting systems, and complaint procedures.[75]

The American customer service movement is one of the most robust (in terms of experiments launched) and least developed (in terms of knowledge and concepts).[76] Part of the problem is that citizens are "owners" of government as well as service recipients, NPR's critics pointed out.[77] Moreover, many government services do not share the basic private sector customer-provider relationship; government usually has no choice about whether to provide key services, and citizens often have no choice about whether to go to government for those services. It is the choice element that drives customer service in the private sector: Companies can decide which products to build and market, and customers can decide which products they prefer—if indeed they choose to purchase any product at all. Thus companies have strong incentives to build and service products that bring them the greatest profit, and customers have strong incentives to patronize companies that provide the greatest satisfaction. Citizens typically cannot choose which fire department or social security business to patronize, and the fire department cannot choose to go into the social security business. Lack of choice dramatically limits the options on both sides of government's service equation and thus reduces critical incentives for efficient and effective service delivery.

Therefore in government customer service has become more a metaphor than a process. It is difficult to argue with the notion that government ought to do whatever it can to make its services more responsive and to make citizen–government interactions less painful. For example, government can accommodate itself to citizens' work schedules by making the hours and locations for driver's license bureaus more flexible. Tax forms and instructions can be designed to be easier to understand. However, the customer service movement runs headlong into the fact that neither side typically has choice in whether to have a relationship in the first place, especially for core government services. Citizens have one set of expectations when receiving services: quick, friendly, convenient service. They usually feel quite differently when paying for services—especially when the services benefit someone else.

The private sector has not cracked this dilemma either. The corporate landscape is littered with spectacular marketing failures, from the Edsel to "new Coke." Many of the core problems and methods are remarkably uniform between government and the private sector: identifying the customer, determining how best to measure success in achieving policy goals, and balancing the overall mission with the specific needs and demands of customers. Indeed, customers can have multiple, even conflicting expectations.[78] However, because of diminished choice in government services and the power that government necessarily exercises over individuals' lives, customer service tactics present substantially more difficult problems in the public sector. The bottom line for democratic government is accountability—not profits or citizen satisfaction—and customer service does not provide a good proxy measure for accountability.

A 1999 survey of customer service in the U.S. federal government indicated that government agencies generally compared favorably with private organizations that had similar missions. The University of Michigan Business School's National Quality Research Center has been surveying private-sector customers since 1994, and the 1999 survey represented the first application of their methodology to government. On a 100-point scale, the average customer satisfaction score for private sector service businesses was 71.9; government agencies scored a nearly identical 68.6. "Government employees who have contact with the public receive high marks for courtesy and professionalism."[79]

Customer service has played an important role in government reform. In many countries citizens have received a powerful signal that government is interested in improving its service to and relationship with its citizens. Customer service also has transformed the behavior of government officials; it has shaken them out of their bureaucratic routines and focused them on citizens' needs. Some managers have found customer service a useful tactic for breaking down bureaucratic walls and attacking the boundary-spanning problem. However, at its core customer service is somewhat of an enigma. As a reform tool it is both one of the most universal and one of the hardest to define and implement in government.

Unlike private companies, government agencies typically cannot choose their customers. In many government programs, especially taxation and regulatory programs, citizens cannot choose whether to deal with government. Therefore private sector comparisons are suspect; however, the overall approach has been useful in changing bureaucratic behavior.

Information Technology

The computer revolution spread hand in hand with the global revolution in government management.

SPANNING BOUNDARIES. The promise of information technology lies in its ability to easily traverse organizational boundaries and allow quick, easy connections between citizens and government, regardless of which agencies are in charge of providing which services. In many ways technology is the ultimate boundary-spanning technique. Consider the following examples gathered from around the globe.

—In the United States the Social Security Administration has made estimates of individuals' projected benefits available online at its web site (http://www.ssa.gov/oact/anypia/).

—Electronic filing of U.S. income tax returns became popular quickly, and taxpayers can download forms and instructions from the IRS web site (http://www.irs.gov/forms_pubs/index.html).

—Denmark introduced a "paperless" income tax system, in which taxpayers do not have to file paper returns. The government reviews their earnings, calculates the taxes due, subtracts payments withheld from their salaries, and mails them a statement. Taxpayers due refunds receive a check along with the statement. If they owe more taxes, the amount due is rolled into the next year's withholding. If they want to make corrections to the statement, they can do so by telephone or online.[80]

—Qatar created an award-winning national geographic information system based on information supplied from global positioning satellites.

The information supports everything from land use planning to health assessments.[81]

—In Australia's Victoria state, citizens can use the Vic Roads kiosk project to register cars and obtain driver's licenses. (Kiosks are self-operated electronic systems stationed in public areas, such as shopping malls and building lobbies, that allow citizens to conduct business without having to visit government offices or deal directly with government officials.) The system brings not only convenience but also power to citizens, because it eliminates what surveys have shown to be the greatest complaint about traditional licensing procedure: unflattering photos. Vic Roads allows drivers to pick the picture they like best. In a country as vast as Australia, government officials have concluded, such electronic systems conquer "the tyranny of distance" and improve citizens' access to government. In addition government officials do not have to be stationed in every small community throughout the country.[82] The systems, which have spread throughout Australia's state and local governments, allow government to customize services to citizens as well as save money.

—Sweden's Kista project seeks both vertical and horizontal integration of services: across both a range of services and a range of providers, regardless of whether they are national or local.

—Finland has centralized some judicial services once provided by municipalities to permit information technology to improve the system.[83]

—Britain's "life events" system, an effort to organize government services not by agency but by event or transaction, seeks to present a seamless view of government, regardless of which level or branch of government provides the service.

CENTRALIZATION FOR COORDINATION. Many information technology innovations are inherently centralizing. "Coordination," the OECD explains, "occurs at the point of service delivery."[84] To make things work seamlessly at the bottom, they must be carefully coupled from the top. Computer systems must be technically compatible and must rely on carefully integrated databases. The more local governments or individual national government agencies construct their own systems and build their own hardware, the greater the chance that the systems cannot easily be linked. Building effective links requires making—and sharing—basic decisions about systems, software, and database construction.

Other forces have enhanced and continue to enhance this trend toward centralization. As information technology became more central to the European Union, the member states looked for basic standards to ensure the compatibility of their data. Similarly, fear of the potential havoc that the Y2K computer "bug" could wreak led many countries to share information and implement solutions so that their systems would continue to operate beyond December 31, 1999. Information technology is not cheap, and the orders often have come from high levels of government that, in return for their investment, have insisted on certain system standards.

TECHNICAL DIFFICULTIES AND CHALLENGES. Not surprisingly, big problems have accompanied the spread of computer-based systems. New York's new system to encode government food and benefits credits on electronic debit cards has suffered serious growing pains. Banks imposed large fees on users, which eroded the value of the benefits. Many automatic teller machines (ATMs) refused to accept the cards, and the cards did not always work. Recipients complained that too many merchants do not accept them. Consequently, some recipients retreated to storefront check-cashing services that charge even higher fees.[85]

The problems in New York have not prevented other states from launching their own computer-based systems for public assistance. The California Department of Social Services, for example, planned its own ATM system to improve both the public assistance program's efficiency and the lives of recipients. "We're trying to remove the stigma of public assistance," explained Sidonie Squier, a spokeswoman for the agency. "[Beneficiaries] will swipe their cards at the [merchant's] check stand just like the rest of us. It should be an esteem builder."[86]

The new technology has been very popular in some applications. In Britain, citizens have liked photo driver's licenses because, as in the United States, they are useful for a wide range of other identification uses. (In California, for example, people who do not drive can request a nondriver's license—a government-issued photo identification card.) Indeed, eleven of the fifteen European Union countries have issued identification cards.[87] The European Union also is planning to issue medical smart cards, which would electronically encode information about an individual's blood type, medical history, and other medically useful information.[88]

Privacy concerns also have plagued these ambitious technology plans. For example, early in 1999 the British government proudly announced a new "smart card" for citizens. Within a decade citizens would be able to use this card to conduct all of their business with government. However, the government slowed its implementation because citizens were worried that sensitive personal information might leak out of the system. In the United States, citizens in some states have led a campaign to prevent the disclosure of name, address, and telephone information in department of motor vehicles files. They generally are public records and thus can be viewed by anyone, but some states were selling the information to telemarketers. State legislators are debating proposals to allow citizens to request that the information not be disclosed.

Computer systems present complex technical issues. It is one thing to create systems; it is often quite another to make them work reliably and predictably for citizens across borders and, sometimes, with different languages. Even more important, the spread of information technology raises daunting privacy issues: Which information will government collect? Who will have access to the information? How can information be sped to those who ought to have access to it while keeping it out of the hands of those who ought not? These difficulties present both short-term and some long-term problems for what surely will be a continuing trend in government services. Information technology not only provides a boundary-spanning bridge; "technology itself is a change agent."[89] It inevitably will change how government does what it does and how government employees understand their roles.

Regulatory Reform

Underlying all of these reform tactics in most nations has been a commitment to reduce government regulation. South Korea abolished almost half its regulations. Costa Rica struck down entry barriers to the pharmaceutical industry.[90] The European Union has worked to coordinate regulations among its members. For example, it has worked to reduce approvals in each country for pharmaceuticals and to encourage single permitting for a wide range of commercial goods. Deregulation of the telecommunications and transportation industries has cut prices and spurred job creation in countries ranging from Japan and Finland to the United States and Germany. New Zealand abolished almost all agricultural support in the mid-1980s in the midst of the government's other reforms. Unemployment increased and some businesses failed, but within a decade the agricultural sector became internationally competitive and now contributes more to the economy than ever before. Deregulation of the Swedish taxi industry increased the supply and decreased waiting time. In Japan, telecommunications deregulation reduced prices by 41 percent.[91]

Deregulation is scarcely an immediate and automatic winner. Markets grow according to the rules in which they exist; changing the rules shifts the balance among the players and creates different winners and losers. Moreover, the New Zealand case shows that restructuring markets can take some time and, in the meantime, impose substantial costs. Thus on one level, deregulation is about economic efficiency. But on another level, it is quite clearly about politics and political redistribution. For these reasons an OECD assessment found that "the most important ingredient for successful regulatory reform is the strength and consistency of support at the highest political level. Ministers have a direct role to play in assuring that strong political leadership will overcome vested interests in both public and private sectors which benefit from the status quo and resist beneficial change."[92]

The political stakes of regulation and deregulation make piecemeal reform difficult and economically risky. Piecemeal reforms can stir up substantial political battles at each turn without fundamentally transforming the markets. The most successful regulatory reforms have been comprehensive instead of piecemeal.[93]

In many ways regulation is the prototypical symbol of traditional government. By contrast deregulation has been a critical foundation of reform since the late 1970s. Its roots are partly economic; that is, they use market forces to replace bureaucratic decisions. They are even more fundamentally political, because they uproot long-established interests worldwide that have shaped the rules of the game to their benefit. Attempting to separate deregulation's political roots from its economic and administrative instruments is to dismiss much of what is most interesting about this tool. Indeed, this is the most important lesson for the other reform tactics as well.

Policy, Management, and Governance

The tactics of the global reform movement sought to reduce government's costs, make government a friendlier partner to both citizens and businesses, improve government managers' ability to manage, and improve the productivity of government. It was an ongoing effort to make government "work better and cost less," according to the NPR. Reformers around the world have celebrated their accomplishments but soberly have taken account of two basic problems. New Zealand's Prime Minister Jenny Shipley argued after her nation's fifteen years of reform experience,

"There is still much to do." She continued, "No government, no economy, can stand still. Reinventing government does not stop. It must be continual, forever demanding new benchmarks of performance to define value and improvement for people." And she noted, "Reform fatigue and the power of vested interests will always be formidable obstacles."[94]

The fact that reform is never finished has been the most important lesson of the strategies and tactics of management reform. The reform movement has centered on administrative tools. In the end these tools have meaning only to the degree that they advance political goals, and they have little power without political support. As I show in the next chapter, reform is deeply embedded in governance.

CHAPTER FOUR

Reform as Governance

The management reform movement dominated governments around the world in the last decades of the twentieth century. The level of activity, from New Zealand's vigorous efforts to reshape the state to those of many developing countries to speed their own transformations, was simply remarkable. Perhaps never before had so many governments tried to change so much so fast.

Assessing whether those reforms produced solid results is a different matter. Cynics dismissed many of the efforts as the latest fad. Indeed, the continual march of budgeting reforms, from planning-based program budgets through zero-based budgets to quality- and results-driven budgets, fueled the cynics' claims: Near-constant reforms often seemed to breed only more reforms. Moreover, good data on what governments have attempted, let alone what they have accomplished, often have been scarce. Reformers have been too busy with their efforts to chart their results. The paucity of data sometimes has been a boon to elected officials, because it became difficult to contest their claims of success. At other times the fuzzy data have provoked political disputes over which reform claims are legitimate and which are overstated. For example, in 1999 a General Accounting Office report questioned $137 billion in cost savings claimed by the NPR. Representative Dan Burton (R-Ind.) accused the Clinton administration of working "to pad the numbers" and of "reinventing accounting rules." One administration official countered,

"These are savings that took place," and concluded, "We frankly are proud of that."[95]

What impacts have these reforms had? How have the big issues varied in less developed nations? These issues frame the questions addressed in this chapter.

Basic Puzzles

Few if any government leaders launched management reforms to improve administration and service delivery. These goals were important, but only in the context of aggressive efforts to save money. In most nations, it was the combination of the "works better" and "costs less" elements that drove the reforms. However, gauging the cost savings of the reforms has been very difficult everywhere, for several reasons. First, it is impossible to know what decisions governments otherwise would have made, so there is no solid baseline for comparison. Second, despite many nations' investment in better cost accounting, most public accounting systems remain inadequate to the task of tracking the real cost of government programs and the links between inputs and results. Third, the management reforms were entangled in ongoing, high-profile political decisions and, often, pitched political battles. Separating the management from the political issues usually was impossible, as the dispute between Representative Burton and Vice President Gore showed. Indeed, the management reforms typically got the greatest attention when they yielded politically important results. Such is the paradox of assessing the management reforms: They became most visible and important as they became less separable from political forces.

Comparative analysis of the leading administrative reform efforts suggests that the leading reformers showed impressive gains in productivity. Analysis was incomplete at best, but anecdotal evidence, coupled with cross-national comparisons, indeed suggests that many nations succeeded in improving government's ability to produce more and better government services at lower cost.[96] However, no good, reliable data are available in any country regarding the savings that the reforms produced. What is the strongest indicator of success? Many nations (especially New Zealand, the United Kingdom, and the United States) have persevered in the reform effort, despite pitched political battles and, in New Zealand and the United Kingdom, changes in government.

Size of Government

In many nations one of the goals of the reform movement was to reduce the size of the public sector. Many of the nations with the most aggressive reform efforts saw reductions in government spending as a share of the economy during the 1990s (figure 4-1). Spending by New Zealand governments, for example, fell 18 percent, to 40 percent of gross domestic product (GDP). American spending (at all levels of government) shrank more than 8 percent to 32 percent of GDP. Other governments with more modest reforms, such as Germany, Japan, and South Korea, tended to spend more. Japanese government spending grew 27 percent (to 40 percent of GDP), and South Korean spending increased 49 percent (to 27 percent of GDP).[97] In general, governments with more aggressive reforms tended to reduce their spending more as a share of the economy (table 4-1).

These numbers raise as many cautions as they suggest conclusions. There is no correlation between the size of government and the scope of reform efforts. Indeed, Sweden, which launched some of the world's most comprehensive budget reforms, leads the industrialized world in government spending. Spending shrank only slightly in the 1990s, by 1 percent; the government had launched the reforms to avoid slashing the nation's welfare state. Management reform is not associated with any particular size of government (as measured by government spending as a percentage of the economy). In fact, spending by the American government before reforms was substantially smaller than by those in New Zealand and the United Kingdom after reforms. (Government spending typically is measured in comparison with the size of the domestic economy [GDP].)

The ratio can change as a result of budget cuts or economic growth. These changes measure both the shrinkage of government and the economic growth that many nations enjoyed in the 1990s. The universal goal of reformers was to grow the private economy. Separating the impact of government reforms from other changes that fueled economic growth is an extremely difficult issue that, at best, will require many more years and far more data to assess. In general government management reforms were driven by political imperatives to fuel economic growth and accommodate government spending. The political results of the reforms—perhaps measured best by elected officials' willingness to continue to press ahead—is perhaps the most useful proximate measure of the reforms' success.

Figure 4-1. *Change in Government Outlays as a Percentage of GDP,*
1990–2000

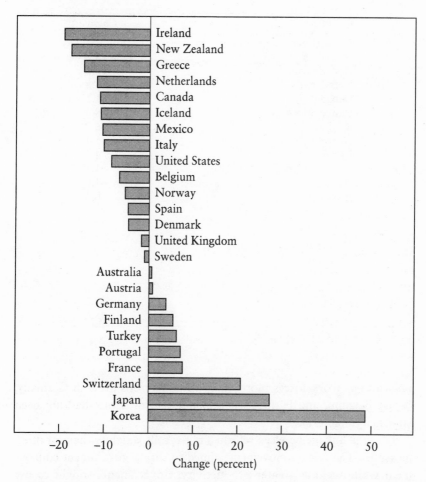

Change (percent)

Source: Analytical Databank, OECD.

How did management reforms affect government payrolls? The compensation of government employees (measured as a percentage of GDP) fell in most nations during the 1990s. It fell most in the nations that engaged in the most aggressive reforms (figure 4-2): In the United Kingdom government payrolls decreased by more than one-third, and in New Zealand they decreased by 14 percent. As with government spending, governments that conducted more aggressive reforms tended to

Table 4-1. *Change in Government Outlays as a Percentage of GDP,
1990–2000*

Country	Change
More aggressive reformers	
Ireland	–19.2
New Zealand	–17.6
Netherlands	–11.8
Canada	–11.1
United States	–8.5
Belgium	–6.7
Norway	–5.4
Denmark	–4.6
United Kingdom	–1.7
Sweden	–1.0
Australia	0.6
Finland	5.4
Switzerland	20.7
Less aggressive reformers	
Germany	3.8
Portugal	7.1
France	7.6
Japan	27.2
Korea	48.6

Source: Analytical Databank, OECD.

reduce their work forces more. In contrast payrolls grew in Germany,
Japan, Belgium, and France, where major reform efforts had not been
launched (table 4-2).[98]

Thus the linkage between reform and payrolls is tighter than for other
measures. The reform movements aimed to shrink government employment while seeking greater productivity. Governments sought to use
fewer employees to maintain or even improve their levels of service. If
measuring savings is hard, then assessing the impact on the quality of services is even harder. At least it is clear that many governments shrank
their overall spending and their payrolls as a share of their national
economies.

Trust in Government

In most nations the reformers quite explicitly pledged to improve their
citizens' trust in government. Although the decline of civic trust in

Figure 4-2. *Change in Government Employee Compensation as a Percentage of GDP, 1990–97*

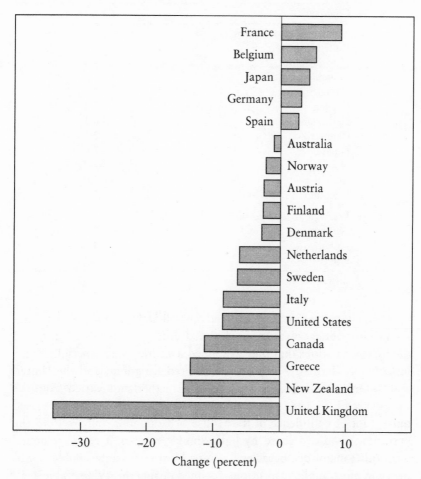

Source: Analytical Databank, OECD.

American government is well-documented,[99] cross-national comparisons are difficult because researchers rarely have asked the same questions in the same way at the same times. However, in many nations researchers have found similar, troubling trends through research such as the World Values Survey. In almost all industrialized nations, citizens' responses indicate declining confidence in public institutions. The drop has been especially sharp in Germany, Japan, Italy, the United States, and even Sweden.[100]

Table 4-2. *Change in Government Employee Compensation as a Percentage of GDP, 1990–97*

Country	Change
More aggressive reformers	
United Kingdom	–34.2
New Zealand	–14.4
Canada	–11.3
United States	–8.6
Sweden	–6.4
Netherlands	–6.1
Denmark	–2.8
Finland	–2.6
Norway	–2.2
Australia	–1.0
Belgium	5.3
Less aggressive reformers	
Germany	3.1
Japan	4.3
France	9.1

Source: Analytical Databank, OECD.

Robert Putnam, Susan Pharr, and Russell Dalton reported that confidence in political institutions declined during the 1990s in eleven of the fourteen nations that they examined. Declines were especially sharp in Canada, Germany, Sweden, the United Kingdom, and the United States. Only Denmark, Iceland, and the Netherlands varied from the overall trend. In 1985, for example, 48 percent of Britons expressed quite a lot of confidence in the House of Commons, but by 1995 the percentage had decreased by half. Similar or greater results plagued most other major democracies.[101] Pippa Norris found that public confidence in most public institutions declined during the 1990s (table 4-3). Citizens remain committed to democracy as a form of government, but they are unhappy about the way it is operating in their own countries. This discontent, claims Norris, has proven a powerful engine driving the reform of government.[102]

On the surface these and similar survey results are scarcely a ringing endorsement of government reform. There is no evidence that the extensive management and political reform efforts have halted the downward slide of public confidence in government. However, it is likely that public

Table 4-3. *Changes in Citizen Opinions of Government Performance in the 1990s*

Performance area	Number of countries		Overall mean percentage change
	Increasing	Decreasing	
General system performance (N = 12)	4	8	–7
Confidence in parliament (N = 22)	3	15	–12
Confidence in government (N = 9)	3	5	–12
Satisfaction with the democratic process			
European Union (N = 15)[a]	7	4	–0.3
Central and Eastern nations (N = 18)	7	7	0.0

Source: From analysis by Pippa Norris, "Mapping Political Support in the 1990s: A Global Analysis," in Pippa Norris, ed., *Critical Citizens: Global Support for Democratic Governance* (Oxford University Press, 1999), table 2.15.

a. The mean is heavily skewed by Portugal's 35.5 percent decrease. If Portugal is removed from the sample, the mean is a 2.4 percent increase.

confidence is a lagging indicator of reform; it might take long and sustained governmental improvement to register with citizens and to be reflected in higher confidence in government. The decline of government began decades before the global movement in management reform started. In many countries, the reform effort began as part of a broader strategy to reverse the trend. At the least, the global reform movement is a symptom of—and a reaction to—the decline of public confidence in governmental institutions and performance.

Assessment

Any assessment of the global reform movement is ultimately unsatisfying. Despite efforts that span years, even decades, clear indicators of success are hard to find. The administrative efforts inevitably are tied up with political decisions. Citizens seem to trust their institutions less than they used to, but whether the reform movement has helped close the confidence gap is unclear. Moreover, it is difficult, if not impossible, to separate confidence in elected decisionmakers from confidence in the unelected administrators who carry out their decisions.

Two strong characteristics of the administrative reform movement demonstrate its power. First, the movement has spread throughout much of the world. Government officials champion reform because they believe it is likely to help. Second, no government that has launched such a reform movement has ever given up on it. Although changes of government brought shifts in strategy and tactics, throughout the 1990s there never was a retreat. Government officials continue to try reform because they seem to believe it gives them political leverage—and perhaps because the managerial challenges of modern government leave them no choice.

Challenges for Developing Nations

Developing nations have embraced reform to help cope with governance problems and to speed the development process. Their problems have been substantial. Public officials from Ghana, for example, talk passionately about their need to shrink the size of government to improve its efficiency, reduce taxes, and stimulate the growth of the private sector. Accomplishing this goal means reducing the government payroll and privatizing government services. However, the government has long been a major source of employment in the country, and reducing the payroll before creating new private sector jobs would increase unemployment. The government has debated privatization, but it is difficult to spin off public enterprises before the private sector has the capacity—financially and managerially—to absorb them. Moreover, this new form of government requires managerial skills among government employees that are in short supply. Government officials feel they have little choice but to move quickly along this road; to do otherwise is to risk slipping behind in the global race for capital and economic growth. Thus they face the task of reinventing their government while inventing and strengthening basic social institutions.

It is little wonder that the reformers' experience, especially in New Zealand, has had such appeal. The World Bank and other international organizations have touted the New Zealand reforms. New Zealand reformers themselves have been missionaries, traveling around the world to talk about what they accomplished. Their ideas are attractive, especially because they have successfully moved the New Zealand economy from stagnation to strong growth. Although the rhetoric of the reforms has spread around the world, Schick has found that only a handful of industrialized nations and just a few developing countries (for example,

Mongolia) have pursued the essential features of the system. Why? Schick argues, "On the whole, industrial and developing countries have not implemented such reforms because the reforms are beyond their reach or do not fit their current needs."[103]

Preconditions for Reform

Schick quite persuasively argues that New Zealand has contributed a great deal to both the theory and practice of public management. However, making the reforms work depends on "important preconditions" that many developing nations—even some industrialized nations—do not possess.[104] The New Zealand experience, as well as the prescriptions of many other reformers, requires a careful match with the capacity of both public and private institutions. In short, management reform is a matter of integrating administrative efforts with the fabric of each nation's government and civil society. Enrique Iglesias, president of the Inter-American Development Bank (IADB), observed, "We do not question whether we need more or less state intervention. It is not a matter of simply downsizing but of rightsizing. The key, as we all know, is the quality of government."[105]

World Bank president James D. Wolfensohn contends that development and reform depend on four structures:

—*Good governance.* "You have got to have governments that have the capacity, have trained people, have clear and transparent laws, and where there is a confrontation at the very highest level of issues of corruption. If you don't have that, you have very little chance of succeeding in your development exercise."

—*A justice system that works.* "You need laws that protect property rights, you need a contract system, you need bankruptcy laws, you need protection of human rights, varying with the country, and you need a justice system that will be clean and honest."

—*A financial system that works.* "Particularly after [the financial crises in] Indonesia and Thailand and South Korea and Mexico and many others, . . . you had better be sure you have a financial system that works—not just financial institutions, but a financial system that is supervised, monitored, controlled, and with people on both sides who are trained."

—*A social system that works.* "You need a social system . . . that can protect the weak, the old, the children, the disabled and can do something for the people who are out of work. That social system need not be an

American-style social system, or British or German—it can be a tribal system, a familial system—but you need to have something that can take care of people who are suffering or aged."

A country without these four structures, Wolfensohn concluded, is "like a rowboat with a big hole in it." He added,

> It is impossible, for example, to privatize in a nation without a well-developed system of competitive markets. New Zealand–style management-by-contract systems—or, indeed, any system of public sector contracting out—cannot work in a society without a well-developed system of contract law. Output-based management controls fail if the government does not have a strong budgeting system to set goals and an accounting system to track results. The government reform movement puts especially heavy pressure on government managers, who not only must do more with less. They must also build new capacity to find imaginative ways to do things they have never done before.[106]

In short, public management reform is not only a job for the public sector. The central reform strategies require broad participation from members of society in setting goals and, in many cases, close partnership between the governmental and nongovernmental sectors. Schick has argued that efforts to reform government that are out of sync with norms elsewhere in society are doomed to fail. "The emergence of open, robust markets is as much a precondition for modernizing the public sector as it is for developing the private economy," he concludes. "It is highly unlikely that government will operate by the book when rules and regulations are routinely breached in private transactions." Especially in many developing countries, Schick contends, the culture of both government and the private sector is informal. Citizens and public officials alike must cope with red tape, rule-bound bureaucracies, bad policies, and poor government performance. Informality can help everyone cope with such systems. However, informality also can breed corruption and more inefficiency and can frustrate efforts to impose management reforms of the sort popularized elsewhere.[107]

New Zealand's contract-driven system is the most formalized governance system in the world. The stunning transformation of the New Zealand economy, even though performance lagged in the late 1990s, lured many governments to consider mimicking its tactics. So too did the dramatic downsizing of its government. Without first building a private sector with the capacity to follow the public sector reforms and developing a more formal and transparent system of governance, Schick warns, developing countries risk "taking shortcuts that turn into dead ends."[108] His warning is not a prescription either for the status quo or for a go-slow process. Singapore and Chile moved rapidly to advance both economic development and public management. Singapore moved from traditional line-item budgets to a system that incorporated important elements of the New Zealand system. The lesson for developing nations is that the public sector cannot be reformed without reforming the private sector in tandem.

Policy and Management

Despite large-scale government downsizing, reformers nevertheless believed firmly in a strong, important role for government. Unlike some doctrinaire conservatives who sought simply to shrink government as much as possible, the reformers were pragmatists who believed that government has an important role to play in society but that the government needs to play its role in a different way. Canada's Clerk of the Privy Council and Secretary to the Cabinet Jocelyne Bourgon argued, "Less government is not a guarantee of better government."[109] Indeed, Iglesias stated, "We do not necessarily believe that government should govern less nor should it try to govern with fewer resources. The pivotal role of the private sector, the engine of growth, is not the answer to all of society's problems."[110]

The quest for reform often has meant redefining government's role. In Bolivia the government has expanded citizens' access to basic services, such as electricity and telephone service. It has developed "four pillars": opportunity, equity, strengthening of governmental institutions, and dignity. Minister of Housing and Basic Services Amparo Ballivain explained, "The steps taken in my country include the rolling back of the state from controlling what we call the 'commanding heights of the economy' to acting as a facilitator." The government has privatized publicly owned enterprises and has worked to shift government's role toward promoting market-driven growth.[111] The Polish government has pursued similar reforms, built on the principle of subsidiarity: devolution and decentralization of government power to bring it closer to the people and enhance the ability of the private sector to perform well.

Reform: Convergence or Divergence?

The management reform movement has spread around the world with remarkable speed. Reformers in every nation have pursued this movement in different ways, with bold rhetoric about reinvention and reform tailored to the special managerial and political problems that face them. However, as I suggested in chapter 2, the reforms have tended to originate in one of two fundamentally different philosophies: Westminster or American.[112]

The Westminster-style strategy began by redefining what government ought to do. It led to the privatization of functions that officials concluded government could or should no longer do. It brought about new budgeting and personnel policies along with reengineering and internal contracting strategies. The Westminster governments have launched sweeping, comprehensive reforms that have sought to restructure government and what it does, from top to bottom.

The American-style strategy sought cheaper, more effective government without shrinking the scope of governmental activities. It has attempted to incorporate the best practices of businesses into government's operations, from customer service to a focus on results. Its reforms have been incremental rather than sweeping and comprehensive.

The Nordic countries have combined these two approaches in their quest for the same goal. They have used sweeping budgetary reforms characteristic of Westminster-style reform to sustain the basic welfare state. However, their efforts were consistent with the broad American strategy to avoid fundamental transformations in the scale and scope of government.

Graham Scott, the architect of the New Zealand reforms, has argued that these two strategies may be converging. He suggests, "For most of the world, the late twentieth century has been about reducing the scope of government. But this process must inevitably slow down." At some point, government will shrink to the point it cannot—for political, economic, and pragmatic reasons—be shrunk any further. All governments eventually will reach a size at which they are likely to stay. At that point, the nations will face the common problem of making their government programs work better and cost less. Scott concludes, "Over time, the rest of us will look more and more like the United States, as the problems of what the government is going to do become less urgent and we deal with them by marginal adjustments rather than sudden and radical change, and focus more on the steady processes of improvement around the organizations that will persist."[113]

The Case for Convergence

Scott's argument focuses on several important issues. With the spread of public management innovations, is the reform movement increasingly centered on certain core questions? Is there convergence in public management reforms? Are the reforms moving more toward the American experiments?

There is in fact strong evidence for convergence. First, the initial phase of reform in many nations focused on shrinking the size and role of the state. The American downsizing effort, except in the federal civil service, was virtually nonexistent; other nations followed the Westminster approach and conducted substantial privatization. However, in most nations whatever downsizing that is likely to happen has happened. This effort has produced governments of vastly different sizes, but all nations face the task of effectively managing the government that remains. Moreover, more elected officials have made a strong case for a positive role of the government that is left. Many nations are converging on a recognition of the basic problems: the twin puzzles of redefining government's role and size and of building the capacity for making it work effectively. These central issues have driven the Clinton administration's reinventing government campaign.

Second, the reform movement has moved many governments away from a focus on inputs (money spent or people employed by government) to a focus on results (outputs or outcomes). With GPRA, the United States launched perhaps the world's most ambitious results-oriented system. How well government managers can master the program's technical details and how elected officials deal with the results measures is anything but clear, but the system at least creates a novel process. The New Zealand government has led the way in output measurement. Other Westminster nations have developed related systems, from customer-driven measures to private sector–derived benchmarks. Elected officials are unlikely to abandon inputs. In most nations, their job is to define public goals and determine how best to use society's resources. Budgets and public hiring are the coin of the political realm. However, governments are paying far more attention to the results their spending programs bring.

Third, many nations have devolved substantial responsibility for domestic policy to their local governments. In federal systems such as

Australia, Canada, Germany, and especially the United States, such devolution has long been a central part of governance. However, other nations have spun governmental responsibility to lower levels. In the United Kingdom, referendums in Scotland and Wales led to substantial devolution. The Swedish government has given new responsibility to local governments, and the South Korean government has debated more devolution as well. The shift of responsibility for managing programs—and, as in the case of American welfare reform, for shaping policy—has marked many government reform strategies.

Fourth, institutions in civil society, especially private companies and nonprofit organizations, are playing a stronger role in service delivery. In many nations reform meant downsizing, and downsizing brought significant privatization. In the United States the government had relatively few enterprises to privatize, but the government significantly expanded its reliance on private and nonprofit contractors. As other nations sought to increase their own operating flexibility, especially in Canada and Germany, they looked to contractors as well. The use of nongovernmental agents to deliver public services increased significantly in other nations, and the movement showed strong evidence of spreading.

Fifth, government managers are looking for ideas they can adopt—"best practices" derived from other nations and the private sector. The American reinvention movement derived many of its most important elements, especially the strong focus on customer service and information technology, from the experiences of private companies. In fact, Vice President Gore titled his 1997 report on the NPR's progress *Businesslike Government: Lessons Learned from America's Best Companies.*[114] Osborne and Gaebler's *Reinventing Government* celebrated an "entrepreneurial spirit" borrowed heavily from private companies. The authors were quite emphatic that "government cannot be run like a business." However, they identified ten basic principles that "underlie success for any institution in today's world—public, private, or nonprofit."[115] Trading reform ideas often has been troublesome. Reformers have been tempted to pick the ideas they like and ignore the hard ones. They frequently have failed to build the infrastructure required for the most difficult ventures. Governments often borrow from the private sector without stopping to consider the profound differences between them.[116] Moreover, governments have borrowed private sector ideas just as private reformers have found them unworkable or inadequate. With the high-speed communication of the Internet and the heavy pressure for continued cost cutting and improving productivity, the constant search for management ideas will likely continue around the globe.

Points of Divergence

Despite these important points of convergence, important structural differences probably will prevent the American experience from reshaping global management reform. The New Zealand and similar Westminster reforms sought to clarify policy goals, administrative responsibility for achieving those goals, and measures to gauge how well managers achieved those goals. The Westminster reforms gave managers great operating flexibility in exchange for tough accountability for their performance. In practice there often was considerable slippage between the rhetoric and reality. Moreover, few nations were as aggressive as New Zealand in pursuing this framework. Nevertheless the driving logic of the Westminster reforms sought to draw clear lines that defined responsibility sharply: lines between goals and results, between inputs and outputs, and between policymakers and managers.

The American governmental system, by contrast, is built on a constitutional system of separated powers and shared responsibility. Especially in domestic policy, responsibility for program management is shared among the federal, state, and local governments—and between government and its nongovernmental partners. Within government, responsibility for decisions is shared among the three branches. The rough-and-tumble politics of the American system reinforces the constitutional features. These elements would make it difficult for American governments to match the requirements of the Westminster reforms. For the Westminster governments, moving toward the fuzzy responsibilities of the American system would undermine the very reforms they have developed.

In short the Westminster-style reforms build on drawing sharp boundaries. The American system traditionally has existed by avoiding such clear lines. Moreover, the American strategies and tactics of the last half of the twentieth century have blurred existing lines even further. Governments at all levels have relied more on contracting out for projects ranging from defense contracts to social service delivery. The growth of Medicaid and Medicare in the 1970s and 1980s accelerated this trend, and welfare reform in the 1990s brought new nongovernmental partners to the service delivery system. Indeed, American reforms are perhaps most distinctive for their integration of governance deeply into the very fabric of civil society.

The Westminster governments have moved toward the use of civil society in the governance system. Non-Westminster parliamentary systems from South Korea to eastern Europe have considered such a move themselves. In federal systems such systems of shared power have come more easily and have moved more quickly, especially in Australia and Canada. But this issue frames a central puzzle for any notion that the reforms are converging. American reforms are moving toward greater blurring of the responsibilities for policies within government, and of the responsibilities for managing those policies between government and civil society. Despite the growing importance of civil society in other nations, many of the reforms have moved in the exact opposite direction, toward more attempts to clarify the boundaries between policy and administration and between government and society. In fact, the "new public management" (the academic theory that supported Westminster-style reforms) was largely an effort to reinvent the distinction between policymaking and policy execution that American scholars spent most of the twentieth century trying to erase.

The question of convergence and divergence remains very much open. Will non-American systems, especially among the Westminster nations, slide away from their efforts to draw sharp boundaries and more toward American-style shared power? Will American reformers move more toward the agency-style approach of the Westminster governments and give government's agents more responsibility in exchange for greater accountability? The questions that remain guarantee continued debate and ongoing reform. If nothing else, the experience of the global reform movement establishes ongoing reform as the foundation for government in the twenty-first century.

CHAPTER FIVE

Governance for the Twenty-First Century

M ost discussions of public management reform begin with a flawed premise: that management reform is most fundamentally about management. Discussions about the management reform movement often quickly become enmeshed in arcane debates about the relative value of output and outcome measures, strategies for culture change, and the importance of reengineering versus "soft" people-based approaches.

Management reform is not fundamentally about management. Elected officials do not pursue management reform for its own sake but because they believe it helps them achieve a broader political purpose. Efficiency has real value to officials because it can help them reduce taxes or increase services. Effectiveness matters because citizens are less likely to complain about programs that they think work well. Even for the managers, management reform is not only about management. Overwhelming evidence indicates that management reform requires strong political direction and support; experience shows that reform led only by internal reformers is inherently and sharply limited. Managers have little incentive to pay careful attention to performance measures if elected officials do not signal that they, too, are paying attention. Measuring results is always a risky proposition; it can shed unwelcome light on mistakes and draw political attack from those seeking to wound programs they dislike.

The same is true for developing nations, perhaps even more so. Developing nations face the challenge of speeding up their internal economic progress while creating strategies to compete effectively in the global economy. In addition to devising new management strategies, they must transform their political institutions. For political and administrative transformations to succeed, they must frequently build new social structures, legal systems, and market arrangements. Like industrialized nations, they must understand not only what the state can do but what it cannot. Inter-American Development Bank president Enrique Iglesias said,

> Allow me to let you in on a little secret that we have learned in our work in reform of the state. Reform of the state is essentially a political issue. It has succeeded in countries in Latin America where there is a general consensus for the need for change. To accomplish this consensus, and where the Bank can play a catalytic role, it is essential that there be a clear vision and acceptance of the role of the state and its limits. Political leadership and political parties are necessary in order to help articulate the goals of the country and therefore the proper role of the state in pursuit of those goals.[117]

Public management is inevitably about politics. Thus management reform is also about political reform, and political reform cuts directly to the core issues of the relationship between government and society. On one hand, this definition risks making the subject too global to study carefully. But on the other hand, the instinct to consider management as only management rules out the most central issues in defining what reform really is and in shaping how well it works.

Reforming public management is not simply a matter of transforming administration with new structures, processes, and (often fewer) people. The New Zealand reforms required elected officials to focus on what they wanted to accomplish and to trust managers to pursue those goals. Accountability shifted to oversight of the contracts. In the United States GPRA required government managers to define explicitly the goals of their programs. It forced an uncommon discussion about what federal programs ought to achieve. American welfare reform devolved most decisions to the states and substantial operating responsibility to private companies and nonprofit organizations. Although American government had relied heavily on nonprofit organizations to deliver social services for decades, the scope and responsibility of contracting lay far beyond what the government, in the United States or elsewhere, had ever before attempted in social service programs.

Public management reform is about strengthening the ability of elected officials to produce results. It requires strong links between government administrators and elected officials. Moreover, it is not only about reforming the public sector. In some countries, including the United Kingdom and New Zealand, the reforms have involved substantial privatization of government enterprises. The private sector had to absorb these enterprises. It had to expand its traditional services and find new ways of making markets more competitive. In nations from China to Germany, nonprofit organizations are playing a stronger role in the system. Public management reform is as much about politics as management. It is as much about the private and nonprofit sectors as it is about government. To a growing degree, the work of government is only partly work by government. The performance of government strongly depends on the relationship of administration with the rest of government and of government with nongovernmental partners.

Critical Issues in Governance

The reform of government has highlighted critical issues that government must effectively solve and eternal issues that have become far more central.

Nontraditional Service Delivery

A recurring theme of the global government reform movement is the growth of nontraditional, nonhierarchical, and often nongovernmental tactics of service delivery. Of course, governments have long relied on nongovernmental partners. In the United States, the use of nongovernmental partners has become an essential and perhaps irreversible part of the governance system. Other nations, drawn by the impressive success of welfare reform and by the prospect of greater productivity and more flexibility through nongovernmental partners, are increasingly following the American lead. In the twenty-first century government will become increasingly reliant on nongovernmental partners for service delivery, and these nongovernmental partners will depend more on governmental revenue as an important part of their revenue stream. This interdependence will create new challenges for institutional integrity and operating effectiveness for both parties.

More Decentralization to Lower Levels of Government

Pushing operating responsibility to lower levels of government has become a central premise of many government reforms. Sweden has devolved health care programs to local governments. The United Kingdom has devolved most domestic responsibilities to new parliaments in Scotland and Wales. Even relatively centralized and bureaucratized governments such as in South Korea and Japan are considering the expansion of such devolution. Governance in the twenty-first century is likely to devolve yet more policymaking and management responsibility to lower levels of governance. For federal systems, decentralization will bring new challenges in sorting out governmental roles. For unitary systems, it will bring even bigger challenges of determining who is responsible for what.

Increased Burdens of Service Coordination

From the British strategies of one-stop shopping—what the government calls "single window" services—to the extensive American NPR program of customer service, governments increasingly are seeking to improve the coordination of their services. Indeed, one major negative side effect of the agency-based reforms in the Westminster countries is the fragmentation of service delivery. Agencies typically have strong incentives to look to their own programs and weak incentives to work with other agencies that serve the same citizens. Even in the United States, where cross-unit, cross-government work is commonplace, drawing managers out of their tunnel vision into a bottom-up view of integrated services is difficult indeed. Governance in the twenty-first century certainly will require efforts to strengthen the ability of government organizations to manage effectively. Just as important, it requires increasing the ability and incentives of government managers to work across their organizational boundaries to make government and its services more seamless and transparent to citizens.

Growing Globalization

The events of the late 1990s clearly demonstrated that governments can no longer operate alone; cooperation and coordination are the name of the game. The multigovernment task force that fought the war in Bosnia required the approval of all the participating governments on everything from broad strategy to specific bombing targets. Though much criticized, the International Monetary Fund played a critical role in attacking the financial crisis in Southeast Asia, and the World Bank has led a strong campaign for reform as part of its strategy for aiding developing nations. When Coca-Cola's drinks in Belgium were contaminated, it found itself dealing most with the European Union's food regulations. Globalization has become more than a watchword. It is unquestionably a central tenet of governance in the twenty-first century: National governments maintain their sovereignty but also must share important decisions with multinational organizations and with other nation-states around the world. Moreover, the multinational organizations—the International Monetary Fund, the World Bank, the United Nations, the European Union, and others—must carefully define their new roles in the global system of governance and develop the necessary capacity to play those roles effectively.

The Role of National Governments

Daniel Bell's prophetic column, which appeared in the *Washington Post* in January 1988, focuses the big issues sharply:

> The problem is a mismatch of governmental responsibilities and structures. Over time problems have tended, sloppily but steadily, to sort themselves out to the level of government best equipped to handle them. Programs that require adaptation to local needs, such as welfare reform, have tended to flow down to local governments. Programs that require multinational cooperation, such as trade policy and peacekeeping, have tended to flow up to international organizations and ad hoc international coalitions.[118]

This gradual accommodation of problems to institutions is only partially under way. At best, a generation of uneasy adaptation lies ahead. Moreover, the fundamental question remains left unanswered: If more policy problems are flowing down to subnational governments and up to multistate organizational forms, what will be the nation-state's role in governance in the twenty-first century? And what capacity does it need to play this role effectively?

Government will need to be centrally involved in at least five key tasks:

—*Managing basic functions:* Central governments will need to continue to provide for the common defense, conduct foreign policy, and perform the other basic functions that define the core of national identity.

—*Redistributing income:* Governments have taken very different views on just how much redistribution is desirable. Regardless of the level of redistribution, low-level governments cannot adequately perform it. Redistribution must begin from a broad base to be effective.

—*Gathering data and promoting information-based linkages:* There is a fundamental paradox in the rapid spread of microcomputers. Although it has democratized information technology much more than in the days of large mainframe computers, communicating effectively across these related systems requires careful planning to ensure seamless integration. Such systems feed off large volumes of data that must be gathered in uniform ways to be effective. Thus central governments have an important role to play in making the information age work.

—*Building bridges:* Management reforms depend heavily on new, close relationships among different government bureaucracies and between government and civil society. Central governments will have to play an effective integrative role to ensure effective public services.

—*Thinking strategically:* To cope with everything from work-force planning to next-generation technology, societies will need institutions that think strategically and shape the investments required to make cutting-edge systems work. It might be asking too much for such strategic thinking to happen spontaneously in the market.

Reform and Governance

The lessons of the global management reform movement are that
—these five key tasks are essential;
—government, especially central government, must play an effective role in completing these tasks; and
—these functions often require different skills among government managers, different processes in government, and sometimes new institutions to make them work well.

If governments are to learn these lessons, they will need to build a constant instinct for reform into their operations and to focus this instinct on building capacity to meet the challenges that lie ahead.

Reform and reinvention are likely to become standard practice for governments of all stripes. Jocelyne Bourgon, Canada's clerk of the Privy Council and secretary to the Cabinet, asked whether we have only scratched the surface of this challenge:

And could it be that we all need to do much more to achieve the full potential of reinventing government, and to achieve the full potential of a modern society, a modern society which is a knowledge economy and a knowledge society, where we want both the fullness and the richness of a market economic system and the fullness and the richness of a democratic society coming together for the benefit of all citizens?[119]

Management reform for the twenty-first century will require the instinct for reform to become hardwired into the practice of government. Ultimately, this strategy means coupling the reform impulse with governance—government's increasingly important relationship with civil society and the institutions that shape modern life.

Notes

1. See, for example, Organization for Economic Cooperation and Development (OECD), *Managing across Levels of Government* (Paris, 1997), p. 15; and Michael Keating, *Public Management Reform and Economic and Social Development* (Paris: OECD, 1998), pp. 13, 54.

2. Allen Schick, *The Spirit of Reform: Managing the New Zealand State Sector in a Time of Change* (Wellington: New Zealand State Services Commission, 1996).

3. The literature on the New Zealand reforms is vast. Of special help, in addition to Schick's analysis, are the following works: June Pallot, *Central State Government Reforms: Report on New Zealand*, report prepared for the Central State Government Reforms Project (Berlin, 1999); Colin James, *The State Ten Years On from the Reforms* (Wellington: State Services Commission, 1998); Graham Scott, Ian Ball, and Tony Dale, "New Zealand's Public Management Reform: Implications for the United States," *Journal of Policy Analysis and Management*, vol. 16 (1997), pp. 357–81; Jonathan Boston and June Pallot, "Linking Strategy and Performance: Developments in the New Zealand Public Sector," *Journal of Policy Analysis and Management*, vol. 16 (1997), pp. 382–404; Jonathan Boston, John Martin, June Pallot, and Pat Walsh, *Public Management: The New Zealand Model* (Oxford University Press, 1996).

4. Schick, *The Spirit of Reform*, p. 12.

5. Scott, Ball, and Dale, "New Zealand's Public Management Reform," p. 360. See also Malcolm Bale and Tony Dale, "Public Sector Reform in New Zealand and Its Relevance to Developing Countries," *The World Bank Research Observer*, vol. 13 (1998), pp. 117–19; and Jonathan Boston, John Martin, June Pallot, and Pat Walsh, eds., *Reshaping the State: New Zealand's Bureaucratic Revolution* (Oxford University Press, 1991). On principal-agent theory, see James Buchanan and Gordon Tullock, *The Calculus of Consent: Logical Foundations of Constitutional Democracy* (University of Michigan Press, 1962); Mancur Olson,

The Logic of Collective Action (Harvard University Press, 1965); Gordon Tullock, *The Politics of Bureaucracy* (Washington: Public Affairs Press, 1965); William Niskanen, *Bureaucracy and Representative Government* (Chicago: Aldine Atherton, 1971); and Terry Moe, "The New Economics of Organizations," *American Journal of Political Science*, vol. 28 (1984), pp. 739-75.

6. Pallot, *Central State Government Reforms*.

7. Boston and others, *Public Management: The New Zealand Model*.

8. Schick, *The Spirit of Reform*.

9. For a comparison, see Donald F. Kettl, "The Global Revolution in Public Management: Driving Themes, Missing Links," *Journal of Policy Analysis and Management*, vol. 16 (Summer 1997), pp. 446-62. The Australian reforms are described in Australian Public Service Commission, *A Framework for Human Resource Management in the Australian Public Service*, 2d ed. (Canberra, 1995). More generally, see David Osborne and Peter Plastrik, *Banishing Bureaucracy: The Five Strategies for Reinventing Government* (Reading, Mass.: Addison-Wesley, 1997).

10. See Peter Aucoin, *The New Public Management: Canada in Comparative Perspective* (Montreal: Institute for Research on Public Policy, 1995).

11. For an analysis, see Sanford Borins, "What the New Public Management Is Achieving: A Survey of Commonwealth Experience," in Lawrence R. Jones, Kuno Schedler, and Stephen W. Wade, eds., *Advances in International Comparative Public Management* (Greenwich, Conn.: JAI Press, 1997), pp. 49-70; Christopher Pollitt, *Managerialism and the Public Services: The Anglo-American Experience* (Oxford: Basil Blackwell, 1990); Colin Campbell and Graham K. Wilson, *The End of Whitehall: Death of a Paradigm* (Oxford: Blackwell, 1995).

12. Pollitt, *Managerialism and the Public Services*, p. 1.

13. Laurence E. Lynn Jr., "The New Public Management as an International Phenomenon: A Skeptical View," in Lawrence R. Jones, Kuno Schedler, and Stephen W. Wade, eds., *Advances in International Comparative Public Management* (Greenwich, Conn.: JAI Press, 1997), p. 114.

14. Borins, "What the New Public Management Is Achieving," p. 65.

15. See Paul C. Light, *The Tides of Reform, 1945-1995* (Yale University Press, 1997).

16. Al Gore, *From Red Tape to Results: Creating a Government That Works Better and Costs Less* (Government Printing Office, 1993).

17. See, for example, Charles T. Goodsell, "Did NPR Reinvent Government Reform?" *Public Manager*, vol. 22 (Fall 1993), pp. 7-10; David Segal, "What's Wrong with the Gore Report," *Washington Monthly*, November 1993, pp. 18-23; Ronald C. Moe, "The 'Reinventing Government' Exercise: Misinterpreting the Problem, Misjudging the Consequences," *Public Administration Review*, vol. 54 (March-April 1994), pp. 125-36. For a balanced analysis, see Peri E. Arnold, *Making the Managerial Presidency: Comprehensive Reorganization Planning, 1905-1996* (University Press of Kansas, 1998) (especially Chapter 12).

18. Peter Drucker, "*Really* Reinventing Government," *Atlantic Monthly* (February 1995), pp. 50, 52. See also Taegan D. Goddard and Christopher

Riback, *You Won—Now What? How Americans Can Make Democracy Work from City Hall to the White House* (Scribner, 1998), p. 49.

19. See David Osborne and Ted Gaebler, *Reinventing Government: How the Entrepreneurial Spirit Is Transforming the Public Sector from Schoolhouse to Statehouse, City Hall to the Pentagon* (Reading, Mass.: Addison-Wesley, 1992); and David Osborne, "Reinventing Government: Creating an Entrepreneurial Federal Establishment," in Will Marshall and Martin Schram, eds., *Mandate for Change* (Berkeley Books, 1993).

20. Bill Clinton and Al Gore, *Putting People First* (Times Books, 1992), pp. 23–24. Quoted in Gore, *From Red Tape to Results,* p. i.

21. Gore, *From Red Tape to Results.*

22. For an explanation of this balance, see Elaine Ciulla Kamarck, "The Impact of Reinventing Government," *The Business of Government* (Washington: PriceWaterhouseCoopers Endowment for the Business of Government, Fall 1999), pp. 18, 20.

23. Bill Clinton and Al Gore, *Putting Customers First: Standards for Serving the American People* (GPO, 1994); and Bill Clinton and Al Gore, *Putting Customers First '95: Standards for Serving the American People* (GPO, 1995).

24. Memorandum from Al Gore to Heads of Executive Departments and Agencies, "Second Phase of the National Performance Review," January 3, 1995.

25. See the NPR web site at www.napawash.org/waiver/index.htm. See also Sydney J. Freedberg Jr., "Attention, Pentagon Shoppers!" *National Journal* (April 25, 1998), pp. 932–33; and General Accounting Office (GAO), *Acquisition Reform: Implementation of Key Aspects of the Federal Acquisitions Streamlining Act of 1994,* NSIAD98-81 (March 1998).

26. NPR Deputy Director Bob Stone, "Gore Official Discusses High-Impact Strategy," *GovExec Daily Briefing* (May 7, 1998) (www.govexec.com/dailyfed [last accessed January 19, 2000]).

27. For a sample of these arguments, see Al Gore, *Businesslike Government: Lessons Learned from America's Best Companies* (GPO, 1997).

28. See John J. DiIulio Jr., Gerald Garvey, and Donald F. Kettl, *Improving Government Performance: An Owner's Manual* (Brookings, 1993), p. 8. See also Goddard and Riback, *You Won—Now What?;* Arnold, *Making the Managerial Presidency;* and especially Paul C. Light, *The Tides of Reform.*

29. Light, *The Tides of Reform.*

30. See the NPR web site at www.napawash.org/waiver/index.htm.

31. Merit Systems Protection Board, *The Changing Federal Workforce: Employee Perspectives* (GPO, 1998), p. vi.

32. Ibid., pp. vi–vii.

33. *National Performance Review Savings for NPR Recommendations Made in 1993 and 1995 as of October 15, 1997* (www.napawash.org/waiver/index.htm [last accessed January 19, 2000]).

34. GAO's assessment of the problem is presented in *Management Reform: Implementation of the National Performance Review's Recommendations,* OCG-95-1 (December 1994).

35. This number excludes employees of the U.S. Postal Service. See U.S. Office of Personnel Management, Office of Workforce Information, *Monthly Report of Federal Civilian Employment*, SF 113-A (January 26, 1998).

36. Ibid.

37. From the Office of Personnel Management Central Data Bank.

38. Paul C. Light, *Thickening Government: Federal Hierarchy and the Diffusion of Accountability* (Brookings, 1995).

39. See Hal Lancaster, "Middle Managers are Back—But Now They're 'High-Impact Players,'" *Wall Street Journal*, April 14, 1998, p. B1.

40. See Perri 6, *Holistic Government* (London: Demos, 1997).

41. See Herbert Kaufman, *Red Tape: Its Origins, Uses, and Abuses* (Brookings, 1977).

42. See Niskanen, *Bureaucracy and Representative Government*.

43. For a comparison, see Kettl, "The Global Revolution in Public Management." This approach formed the core of the "reinventing government" arguments. See Osborne and Gaebler, *Reinventing Government*; and Osborne and Plastrik, *Banishing Bureaucracy*.

44. See Paul C. Light, *The True Size of Government* (Brookings, 1999).

45. For an examination of the tools of government, see Lester M. Salamon, *The Tools of Government* (forthcoming); and Donald F. Kettl, *Government by Proxy: (Mis?) Managing Federal Programs* (Washington: Congressional Quarterly Press, 1988); Frederick C. Mosher, "The Changing Responsibilities and Tactics of the Federal Government," *Public Administration Review*, vol. 40 (November/December 1980), pp. 541-48; and H. Brinton Milward, "The Changing Character of the Public Sector," in James L. Perry, ed., *Handbook of Public Administration* (San Francisco: Jossey-Bass, 1996), pp. 77-95.

46. In fiscal year 1996, for example, almost two-thirds of the federal government's outlays went for checks to individuals—about half in direct payments to individuals (for example, as Social Security and Medicare) and another 15 percent in interest on the national debt. About 14 percent went to state and local governments as grants, some for entitlements (such as Medicaid) and the rest for programs ranging from highway construction to wastewater treatment. About 12 percent was spent through contracts. That left just 11 percent of outlays that the federal government spent directly, and a more than one-third of that amount paid for military personnel.

47. See the OECD web site, www.oecd.org.

48. Al Gore, *The Best Kept Secrets in Government* (GPO, 1996).

49. Treasury Board of Canada, *Getting Government Right: Governing for Canadians* (Ottawa: 1997), pp. 11-15.

50. Prime Minister Tony Blair, *Modernising Government* (London, 1999).

51. Susie Stewart, ed., *The Possible Scot: Making Healthy Public Policy* (Edinburgh: Scottish Council Foundation, 1998); Graham Leicester and Peter Mackay, *Holistic Government: Options for a Devolved Scotland* (Edinburgh: Scottish Council Foundation, 1998). More generally, see Perri 6, *Holistic Government*.

52. Harold Seidman, *Politics, Position, and Power: The Dynamics of Federal Organization* (Oxford University Press, 1998), p. 142.

53. For an analysis of the Canadian reforms, see Sandford Borins, "New Public Management, Canadian Style" (unpublished manuscript, 1999); and Peter Aucoin, *The New Public Management: Canada in Comparative Perspective* (Montreal: Institute for Research on Public Policy, 1995).

54. See Keating, *Public Management Reform and Economic and Social Development*, pp. 18–19.

55. See OECD, *Performance Pay Schemes for Public Sector Managers: An Evaluation of the Impacts* (Paris, 1997), p. 64. The five countries surveyed were Australia, Denmark, Ireland, the United Kingdom, and the United States.

56. Ibid., p. 7.

57. See Patricia Ingraham, Helen Murlis, and B. Guy Peters, *The State of the Higher Civil Service after Reform: Britain, Canada and the United States* (Paris: OECD, 1999); and National Research Council, *Pay for Performance: Evaluating Performance Appraisal and Merit Pay* (National Academy Press, 1991).

58. OECD, *Performance Pay Schemes for Public Sector Managers*, p. 8.

59. National Partnership for Reinventing Government (NPR), *Balancing Measures: Best Practices in Performance Management* (Washington, 1999).

60. The best analysis of these forces is E. S. Savas, *Privatization and Public–Private Partnerships* (Chatham House Publishers, 2000).

61. Keating, *Public Management Reform and Economic and Social Development*, p. 70.

62. Ibid., p. 29.

63. Allen Hepner, *Examining Contestability in the APS [Australian Public Service]: Initial Information* (Canberra: Resource Management Improvement Branch, Department of Finance, 1995) (http://www.dofa.gov.au/pubs/pig/contest/contes02.htm [last accessed January 19, 2000]).

64. Ibid.

65. Jim Flanagan and Susan Perkins, "Public/Private Competition in the City of Phoenix, Arizona," *Government Finance Review*, vol. 11 (June 1995), pp. 7–12.

66. See Savas, *Privatization and Public–Private Partnerships*, pp. 178–79.

67. Donald F. Kettl, *Sharing Power: Public Governance and Private Markets* (Brookings, 1993).

68. Hepner, *Examining Contestability in the APS*.

69. Global Forum, Plenary 1 (January 14, 1999).

70. Clinton and Gore, *Putting Customers First '95*, pp. 1–2.

71. Gore, *The Best Kept Secrets in Government*, p. 33.

72. Keating, *Public Management Reform and Economic and Social Development*, p. 23.

73. *OECD Focus* (http://www.oecd.org/puma/focus/compend/it.htm [last accessed January 19, 2000]).

74. *OECD Focus* (http://www.oecd.org/puma/focus/compend/fr.htm [last accessed January 19, 2000]).

75. Zola Skweyiya, Minister of Public Service and Administration, South Africa, Global Forum, Plenary 1 (January 14, 1999).

76. Keating, *Public Management Reform and Economic and Social Development*, p. 25.

77. See, for example, H. George Frederickson, "Painting Bull's Eyes around Bullet Holes," *Governing*, October 1992, p. 13; Ronald C. Moe, "Let's Rediscover Government, Not Reinvent It," *Government Executive*, June 1993, pp. 46–48, 60; and David Rosenbloom, "Have an Administrative Rx? Don't Forget the Politics," *Public Administration Review*, vol. 53 (November/December 1994), pp. 503–7.

78. NPR, *Balancing Measures*.

79. University of Michigan Business School, American Society for Quality, and Arthur Andersen, *American Customer Satisfaction Index: Federal Agencies Government-Wide Customer Satisfaction Report for the General Services Administration* (December 1999), especially pp. 3, 4.

80. Al Gore, Global Forum, Plenary 2 (January 15, 1999).

81. His Excellency Ali Mohammed Al-Kahter, Qatar's minister of state for Cabinet Affairs, Global Forum, Plenary 2 (January 15, 1999).

82. Honorable Mark Latham, MP (Member of the Australian Parliament), Global Forum, Plenary 2 (January 15, 1999).

83. OECD, *Information Technology as an Instrument of Public Management Reform: A Study of Five OECD Countries* (Paris, 1998), p. 11.

84. Ibid.

85. David Barstow, "A.T.M. Cards Fail to Live Up to Promises to Poor," *New York Times*, August 16, 1999, p. 1.

86. Rebecca Smith, "State Welfare Payments Going the Electronic Route; Debit Cards to Dispense Food Stamps, Benefits," *San Francisco Chronicle*, August 18, 1999, p. A1.

87. "Identity Cards: Politics or Paranoia?" *The Economist*, May 29, 1999.

88. Martin Gallagher, European project manager and coordinator for the "Card Link" project in Europe, and finance director of the Dublin Eastern Health Board, Global Forum, Plenary 2 (January 15, 1999).

89. OECD, Information Technology as an Instrument of Public Management Reform, p. 5.

90. Al Gore, Global Forum, Opening Remarks (January 14, 1999).

91. OECD, *The OECD Report on Regulatory Reform* (Paris, 1997), Table 2.

92. Ibid., introduction (http://www.oecd.org/subject/regreform/report.htm#Introduction [January 19, 2000]).

93. Ibid.

94. Prime Minister Jenny Shipley, Opening Plenary, Global Forum (January 14, 1999).

95. Lisa Getter, "GAO Report Disputes Gore Claims on Red-Tape Cuts," *Los Angeles Times*, August 14, 1999, p. 6.

96. Keating, *Public Management Reform and Economic and Social Development*, p. 32.

97. The figures here include spending for all levels of government. The patterns of government spending vary enormously around the world. In federal systems, state and local governments interdependently raise and spend a substantial amount to fund government programs. In nations with unitary governments, the distribution of spending between national and local governments can vary quite substantially. Hence the best base for comparison among nations is the amount of spending by all governments.

98. The list of nations in the tables is different from those in the figures because of the availability of data.

99. See Joseph S. Nye, Philip D. Zelikow and David C. King, eds., *Why People Don't Trust Government* (Harvard University Press, 1997).

100. See the analysis in "Is There a Crisis?" *The Economist* (July 17, 1999), pp. 49–50.

101. Ibid.

102. Pippa Norris, "Mapping Political Support in the 1990s: A Global Analysis," in Pippa Norris, ed., *Critical Citizens: Global Support for Democratic Governance* (Oxford University Press, 1999), Chapter 2.

103. Allen Schick, "Why Most Developing Countries Should Not Try New Zealand's Reforms," *The World Bank Research Observer*, no. 1 (February 1998), p. 124.

104. Ibid.

105. Luncheon Address, Global Forum, January 14, 1999.

106. Luncheon Address, Global Forum, January 15, 1999.

107. Schick, "Why Most Developing Countries Should Not Try New Zealand's Reforms," pp. 127–28.

108. Ibid., p. 131.

109. Global Forum, Plenary 3 (January 15, 1999).

110. Luncheon Address, Global Forum (January 14, 1999).

111. Global Forum, Plenary 3 (January 15, 1999).

112. A perceptive discussion of this issue is Graham Scott's presentation at the Global Forum, Plenary 1 (January 14, 1999).

113. Ibid.

114. Gore, *Businesslike Government.*

115. Osborne and Gaebler, *Reinventing Government*, p. 21.

116. For a powerful critique of the "borrowing" of reform ideas, see John Micklethwait and Adrian Wooldridge, *The Witch Doctors: Making Sense of the Management Gurus* (Times Books, 1996), especially Chapter 13.

117. Luncheon speech, Global Forum (January 14, 1999).

118. Daniel Bell, "Previewing Planet Earth in 2013," *Washington Post,* January 3, 1988, p. B3.

119. Global Forum, Plenary 3 (January 15, 1999).

Index

bility, 27–28; governance and, 31–35; implementation of reforms, 33; New Zealand reforms, 9, 10, 11–12; performance-related pay, 37–38; political context, 29, 51, 67–69; service integration, 27, 72; U.S. restructuring, 22; Westminster-style reforms, 13–15
Managerialism, 13, 37–38
Marketization, 1–2. *See also* Competition; Westminster model of reform
Mexico, 7

National Partnership for Reinventing Government, 18. *See also* National Performance Review
National Performance Review (NPR), 16, 18, 19–25, 27, 28–29. *See also* United States reforms
Netherlands, 56
New Zealand reform effort, 4, 5, 6; adoption by other countries, 58–59; budgeting and accounting, 36–37; contracting strategies, 39, 60–61; economic theory, 9, 10; future prospects, 12, 48–49; goals, 7; government spending, 52, 53; historical context, 8; management theory, 9, 10, 31; model, 7; motivation, 8–9; performance management, 37, 38, 63; regulatory system, 47, 48; significance, 8; stages, 10; strategies, 10–12; theoretical basis, 9–10. *See also* Westminster model of reform
Nongovernmental organizations, 4, 64, 69; government contracting, 38–41; in reform effort, 69
Norris, Pippa, 56

Office of Management and Budget, 26
Office of Personnel Management, 22
Organization for Economic Cooperation and Development, 35

Output measurement: New Zealand reforms, 11–12; reform strategies, 32, 63; Westminster-style governments, 14. *See also* Government Performance and Results Act

Pallot, June, 10
Performance contracting, 10, 11; United Kingdom reforms, 13
Performance measurement: evaluation of reform outcomes, 50–51, 57; management strategies, 37–38; U.S. reform effort, 19, 26. *See also* Government Performance and Results Act
Pharr, Susan, 56
Poland, 61
Political functioning: governance issues in management reform, 31–35; management reform and, 29, 51, 67–69; and New Zealand reform effort, 9; pressure for reform, 3; regulatory reform effort, 48; state and local elections, 28; U.S. reform effort, 15–16, 17–18, 20, 25, 26; Westminster-style reforms, 13
Pollitt, Christopher, 13
Portfolio budgeting, 36
Postal Service, U.S., 18, 19–20
Private sector, role in reform, 60–61, 64, 69
Privatization, 32, 33, 69; New Zealand reforms, 11; Westminster-style reforms, 14
Procurement system: competition effects, 40; contracting rationale, 38–39; contracting strategies, 38, 39–41, 64; New Zealand reforms, 10; quality of contracted services, 39–40; reform goals, 2; U.S. downsizing effort, 23; U.S. reform efforts, 16–17, 18, 20, 34
Productivity: New Zealand reform effort, 11; reform goals, 1; reform outcomes, 51

Welfare programs. *See* Public assistance programs

Westminster model of reform, 7, 8–10; management structure and function, 13–15, 32, 65, 66; as model for reform, 62–66. *See also* Australia; Canada; New Zealand reform effort; United Kingdom

White, Michael, 28

Wolfensohn, James D., 59, 60

Worker satisfaction, 37

World Bank, 4, 58, 59, 71

World Trade Organization, 4